HOW TO ABANDON SHIP

HOW TO ABANDON SHIP

THE WORLD WAR II CLASSIC THAT CAN SAVE YOUR LIFE

PHIL RICHARDS AND JOHN J. BANIGAN
WITH A FOREWORD BY TWAIN BRADEN

Seahorse Publishing

Foreword Copyright © 2016 by Twain Braden

Skyhorse Publishing books may be purchased in bulk at special discounts for sales promotion, corporate gifts, fund-raising, or educational purposes. Special editions can also be created to specifications. For details, contact the Special Sales Department, Skyhorse Publishing, 307 West 36th Street, 11th Floor, New York, NY 10018 or info@skyhorsepublishing.com.

Skyhorse® and Skyhorse Publishing® are registered trademarks of Skyhorse Publishing, Inc.®, a Delaware corporation.

Visit our website at www.skyhorsepublishing.com.

10 9 8 7 6 5 4 3 2 1

Library of Congress Cataloging-in-Publication Data is available on file.

Cover design by Tom Lau

Print ISBN: 978-1-944824-12-9
Ebook ISBN: 978-1-944824-07-5

Printed in China

Contents

Foreword: Words to Live By

Twain Braden

THE BOOK YOU are holding was first published as an emergency measure to save lives. As such, it needed to be short, clearly written, and furnished with only the bare essentials of knowledge and skill that a young sailor would need to stay alive if he found himself in the water or in a liferaft. The original Introduction provides the grim figures of the numbers of ships sunk and lives lost. As for the ships, they were sunk by torpedoes and bombs; but the crew, unless they were killed upon immediate impact, died because of a lack of preparedness. They jumped into the sea when their ships were still buoyant or into a flaming oil patch in blind panic when they should have mustered patiently at the lifeboats. The book was not written for the ship's officer but for the hundreds of thousands ordinary merchant seamen and enlisted Navy personnel who knew little of the sea and ships.

I was given this book as a joke gift in 1996 when I had my first job as a schooner captain. Twenty-five years old, I was so keenly aware of my youth that I overcompensated with careful notes of preparation, weather forecasts, lists of anchorages, and Plans B for voyage routes, all of which I impressed upon the four-person crew. The mate, a broad-shouldered prankster endowed with great wit, was taking a drag on his cigarette on the quarter deck one afternoon, when, peering at me through the smoke, he handed the book to me. "Got you this," he said. "We might need it." One of the deckhands snickered; the cook smirked.

I tossed it in my bunk and largely forgot about it until, on a foggy day when we were weatherbound, I read through it, amazed at its simplicity and usefulness. Its chapter on navigation alone was well worth the effort, since it reduces the essence of chart-plotting and celestial navigation to third-grade math. ("They are as simple as the directions for a child's game.") The message of the chapter is as pertinent today as wartime 1940s, but for different reasons. Then, the sailors could find themselves in a drifting lifeboat without their officers and their navigational skills; today, we can find ourselves without GPS as a result of failed batteries or, increasingly, a cyberattack on our satellite and communications systems. This is not hyperbole. The world of commercial shipping regards our systems' vulnerabilities to cyberattack as the number-one threat to the bottom line and personnel safety.

Years later I attended a writer's workshop where the author and former *New York Times* columnist Verlyn Klinkenborg discussed the need for clarity in expository writing. He held up this book as a model for neophytes and experienced authors alike. Upon his advice, I used the book as inspiration for writing *The Complete Guide to Sailing & Seamanship*. Dipping into this book at random proves why *How to Abandon Ship* is both a book for salient nautical wisdom as much as words to live by in life:

From Chapter 6, Waterborne: "More likely than not, you will find that enemy sailors will give you the same treatment they would expect to receive." (Cautionary insight of increased relevance as we scrutinize the Geneva Convention in the age of terrorism.)

From Chapter 9, Navigating: "Don't worry your head about what variation is. Concern yourself merely with what you have to do about it. Variation represents an error which you must correct."

And from Chapter 14, Morale: "A dead man's clothes should be distributed among the crew." (This followed a recommended short prayer for burial at sea.)

Some years ago when I was applying for a job as captain of a small passenger vessel, my interview consisted of taking the vessel for a test-sail with the owner and port captain. Before I even went to the wheelhouse I asked to see the lifejackets, bilge pumps, through-hulls, plugs, and fire-suppression system. I put my hands on each piece of equipment and confirmed I knew how it was deployed. (See Chapter 7, Setting Sail.) A few years before, I'd sailed an old schooner from Maryland to Maine, first having to reconstruct the rig from a set of faxed notes. Prior to getting underway we reefed the main, together discussed the weather forecast and intended route, and checked all the through-hull fittings, bilge pumps, and safety gear. (See Chapter 8, Open Boat Seamanship.)

Now, while I still maintain a current captain's license, I use the spirit of preparedness espoused in this book in my law practice. Much of what we do as admiralty lawyers involves responding to sudden crises: a vessel about to sail is in need of immediate arrest for an unpaid chandler's bill; oil seen in the water with the Coast Guard on the way; a tug's crewmember disappeared from the docks in East Boston. On my shelf is a binder replete with checklists for each species of emergency; I revisit and update lists as I gain new experiences. Behind my door hangs a bag with work gloves, flashlight, water bottle, notebook, and a few other sundries, available for a quick response to an on-scene emergency. (See Chapter 1, Prepare Yourself, and Chapter 11, Liferafts.)

It's been more than 70 years since this book was published. Some of the material is dated, such as describing the dangers of jumping overboard while wearing a cork lifebelt. Still, it can be read either for what it is—a pithy manual on sea survival—or as an allegory to life. Prepare, practice, and think before you act, so that when the sky rains fire and the sea boils, you'll grab your proverbial seabag, move quickly to your station, and then, working with compassion and precision as to your comrades' well-being, skillfully deploy the lifeboats.

Twain Braden
Portland, Maine
August, 2016

Acknowledgments

To SCORES OF seamen from torpedoed ships, the authors pay humble tribute for their generous aid in the preparation of this manual.

Space will not permit our giving credit to the great number of sources which have been consulted, but grateful acknowledgment is made to the numerous outstanding authorities on whose work and research we have freely drawn.

We sincerely appreciate the help of Vilhjalmur Stefansson, Arctic explorer; Dr. R. Keith Cannan, Professor of Chemistry, New York University College of Medicine; Dr. Homer Smith,

Department of Physiology, NYU; Dr. Robert Venner, Lenox Hill Hospital; and Dr. William L. Wheeler, Jr.

In the uniformed forces we gratefully acknowledge the help of Rear-Admiral H.L. Brinser, USN; Commander Charles D. Kirk, SC, USN; Lieutenant Commander R. Newton Brown, USNR; Captain Leon Peisachowitz, Med. Res., USA; Captain John Meadows, Ord. USA; Captain Seymour Pond, Army Air Forces; Lieutenant Lawrence Smith, SC, USN; Lieutenant R.J. Stewart, Ord., USA; Lieutenant Max Weiner, Army Air Forces; E. Gould, Chief Pharmacist's Mate, USN; S.G. Morgan, Sr., Chief Inspector of Engineering Materials, USN; Morris Greenberger, Associate Chemist, USN; P.L. Zinna, Associate Inspector of Textiles, USN; and also the interest and information afforded by officials of the Marine Inspection Service.

To Second Lieutenant Edward V. Banigan, Ord. USA, we extend especial acknowledgment for his untiring efforts in having the chapters checked by experts.

Valuable assistance has been rendered by Per Aable, designer of a life suit; Corby Paxton, editor of *The Pilot*; Howard McKenzie, vice president of the National Maritime Union; William B. Hart, associate editor of the American Magazine; T.W. Herbst; S. Londer; and Samuel K. Duff.

We are indebted to William Robinson and Gobin Stair for the speedy and efficient manner in which they prepared the manuscript for publication.

Phil Richards
John J. Banigan
June, 1942

Introduction

THIS MANUAL IS concerned solely with human lives. Its purpose is to aid you to get off a sinking ship and to eventual safety in the best condition possible.

The time has passed when you can indulge in boat-drill lethargy, when you can fiddle with a rope or two while you "let George do it." When a torpedo hits, "George" may prove to be even more panicked and less skilled in launching a life-boat than you, and it may be that he is depending on you to get him safely off the sinking vessel.

Remember that after this war many sunken vessels will be salvaged. But there will be no salvaging the two messmen on the torpedoed tanker *Republic,* who were drowned when they jumped overboard from a ship that did not sink. There will be no salvaging of the *Pan-Massachusetts* seamen who launched a lifeboat into a burning oil slick, or the *City of Atlanta* crew, whose lifeboat, even on the low side, capsized in lowering, costing the lives of eighteen men. Nor will pontoons resurrect the *Allan Jackson* men who were cremated alive within the sheet of fire spreading over the water around their stricken tanker.

Four men on the torpedoed *Malay* died for want of knowledge they could have acquired in ten seconds. They cast off the forward fall first and were flung into the sea. The crew of the Belgian freighter *Gandia* was twenty-six days in a lifeboat. During that time twenty-four men died—because they were not ready for an emergency before it arose.

Within sixty-six hours after the torpedo struck, seventeen men from the Norwegian freighter *Blink* went mad and died. The cause of their death is recorded as exposure. Actually they died from lack of preparation.

Compare the *Blink* tragedy with the case of another Norwegian freighter, the *Nybolt,* torpedoed in the North Atlantic. For nine days during January the survivors were in an open boat. On the eighth day heavy spray covered the boat with an inch-thick layer of ice.

Arne Egenes, surgeon of the *Nybolt,* reported: "In my lifeboat there were twenty-four men. Out of these, twenty-two wore life suits. The two not using the suits were the captain and second mate. The captain died of exposure, and the second mate had to have both legs amputated on account of frostbite."

Most casualties at sea are actually the result of panic, which is the product of ignorance. In a life-or-death emergency you are not going to be entirely free of panic. But you will be able to cut down the fatal intensity of panic if you have previously applied what is offered in this manual to the peculiar circumstances of your own ship and follow these simple don'ts:

Don't depend on peacetime experience and regulations. Keep your eye out for recent and current bulletins issued by the Marine Inspection Service, which has gathered a large amount of data and from it proposed many improvements and changes in safety and lifeboat regulations. Moreover, peacetime regulations do not prevent the operator from acquiring all the safety gear he wants, and the Marine Inspection Service earnestly urges that he secure additional equipment before he is required to do so.

Don't depend on what is in the lifeboat.

Don't stint yourself on safety gear for your own protection. Steamship operators are like all other businessmen— except for providing five thousand dollars of insurance on each seaman, from the captain to the messboy—and they wish to keep expenses at a minimum. So if the steamship operator does not do the supplying, you yourself do the buying. A few dollars from your pocket may mean all the difference between your becoming a 1943 casualty or a 1983 veteran.

Don't let human nature trick you into indifference. A man will readily pay for comfort and a good appearance; but he is reluctant to part with dollars to protect his most precious possession—his own life. The reason for this indifference is plain. He is constantly aware of the benefits of comfort and a good appearance, but death is beyond his experience. He cannot identify himself with it. Death is something that happens to the other fellow.

We earnestly advocate that American seamen urge upon their Congressional representatives and seamen's organizations the advisability of equipping every ship with at least one pair of skates.

A skate is a curved iron, with a narrow edge or runner, which follows the line of the lifeboat from gunwale to keel. The inner part of the skate has a wood lining which fits snugly against the strakes—or fore-and-aft planking—of the boat, and serves to cushion impacts against the ship's side during a launching. The upper part of the skate clamps over the gunwale and the lower part hooks around the keel. The skate is secured on the gunwale either with wooden wedges or fastening screws.

Skates will enable you to launch a lifeboat down the high side with as much as a 46-degree list. Skates protect a lifeboat from being stove in against the side of a rolling ship. Skates eliminate the possibility of a lifeboat capsizing because of extended gangway fittings, rims, bolts, portholes, or plate edges. Forty thousand merchant seamen were killed in World War I. Skates could have saved thousands of them.

This manual is the result of open boat experience in the time of stress, danger, and sudden death. It contains no armchair theory. It is a digest of the lessons learned by the survivors of torpedoed ships.

John J. Banigan, the co-author, was an officer on the *Robin Moor,* the first American vessel sunk by a Nazi torpedo. For nineteen days in a twenty-six-foot lifeboat, Banigan and his crew of ten encountered mountainous seas, tropical storms, doldrums, and blistering equatorial sun. They traveled 898 miles. Yet when they were picked up by the Brazilian freighter *Osorio,* every man was in good condition.

Prepare yourself adequately and, barring a direct hit, you will end up in this war in as good condition as the *Robin Moor* survivors.

Phil Richards
New York City
June, 1942

Chapter 1

Prepare Yourself

THE *HARRY F. Sinclair, Jr.* was still afloat and burning a week after she had been torpedoed. Her fo'c'sle was free from flame, yet men were burned to death because they jumped overboard, and they jumped overboard because they were not prepared.

William Caves, the bosun, safe in a waterborne lifeboat, saw an A.B., who had leapt over the side, struggling in a sea of flaming gasoline. It was impossible to reach the man. Caves saw his shipmate suck fire into his lungs. The A.B. was still fighting while he was being cremated. Then his head nodded briefly as though he were dozing, and Caves watched the charred body float deeper into the flames.

A needless death. The A.B. died because he had no faith in his own seamanship. He did not know the simplest fundamental of buoyancy. (See Chapter 3.) He did not know the treachery of a cork jacket, which is scarcely more of a safety device than a strait jacket.

ADEQUATE DRILLS.—Do not cheat yourself of life the way this tragic seaman did. Prepare yourself, which cannot be done simply by engaging in peacetime boat drills. You are not a lifeboatman unless you have had experience in lowering away. Swinging out is not sufficient. As a boat drill, the mere operation of swinging out has left men inadequately trained, resulting in the loss of many lives during emergencies.

The *Comal Rico* crewmen were prepared. They held a boat drill every other day. When the ship was torpedoed, all survived except two who were killed by a direct hit.

Do not ship out unless you have taken part in a complete abandon-ship drill. Insist on this drill. Joe Melendez from the torpedoed *Saber* reported: "In the nineteen days since we left New York there had been no lifeboat drills." Do not let this situation occur aboard your ships. Complete drills can take place in harbors and when coastwise ships lay up at night and even at sea.

Frank W. Ferguson reported: "I was on the torpedoed *E.M. Clark* as A.B. There were 26 men in my lifeboat and of this number only three were completely familiar with handling a boat. Because of this fact we had a tough time getting clear of the ship."

More drills, more survivors.

LIFE SUIT.—Provide yourself with a life suit. It will protect you against wind, rain, spray, and cold. You can sleep and work in a life suit. In the water it will enable you to get out of the danger area more quickly. It is fire-resisting for at least three minutes. Unless the suit is torn, it will prevent blood from a body wound getting into the water and attracting sharks. The dark color itself will lessen the danger of a shark attack. If the wearer is also clothed in heavy woolen underwear and takes care to keep his circulation active, a life suit will cut down the danger of frostbite and all but eliminate the possibility of death from exposure.

When the *Independence Hall* foundered off Sable Island, the vessel split in two, and a heavy sea prevented the launching of lifeboats. Ten men were lost. Reported Vincent A. Slivjak: "If these men had life suits, their lives would have been saved."

Captain Erling Vorberg, master of the torpedoed Norwegian motor tanker *Barfonn,* reported: "The boatswain, wearing the life suit, was washed into the sea by the first explosion. Due to the weight of the boots, he was kept floating in a standing position by the kapok jacket, even though he was unconscious."

Of the other crewmen who jumped overboard wearing life suits, Vorberg reported: "They were floating around in the water like rubber balls and could easily swim and advance with a rather good speed. When they were picked up in the lifeboats, they were all dry and warm."

In the same convoy, all the men aboard the *Ila* were lost. They did not have life suits. Only two men were saved from the 30 aboard the Greek ship *Evros.* They did not have life suits.

R.G. Wallace, a watertender from the torpedoed *Collamer,* reported: "One man was standing on the poop deck when the well deck was already under water. If this man had a life suit, he would be living today.

"A man was adrift on an old crate, and as close as we could maneuver, the boat was ten feet. We asked him to jump, but he was afraid to do it, and after we drifted away, we heard his cries for a while, but then they were silenced."

INSPECTION.—Inspect the equipment and provisions yourself. Do not take anything for granted. Three days at sea an A.B. aboard the *Jupiter* discovered that the water tanks in four liferafts were dry.

John Larson, A.B. from the torpedoed *Allan Jackson,* reported: "The turnbuckles were frozen and it took anywhere between five and ten minutes to release the gripes."

Julius L. Schwartz from the torpedoed tanker *China Arrow* reported: "Two of the lifeboats had no rudder. The #3 lifeboat was without water."

Do not forget to inspect the screws which hold the mast step in place. In old boats these are sure to be badly rusted. The *Prusa's* #1 boat nearly capsized when the step pulled loose at night while the boat was under full sail.

One of the breakers in the *Prusa's* #1 lifeboat contained a top layer of fresh biscuits, but the balance of the contents was old and moldy.

FIRST AID.—Ashore, you should take a course in first aid; at sea you should practice what you have learned. You should provide yourself with a first-aid manual.

CLOTHING.—Whether you are bound for the Tropics or the Arctic regions, supply yourself with heavy woolen underwear.

CORK PRESERVER.—Do not trust your life to a cork preserver. Men have drowned in them. This type of preserver rides high on the wearer's back, and sometimes it actually forces the head under water. Men who have jumped overboard wearing cork preservers have had ribs, arms, and shoulders broken. The front of the preserver strikes the chin, knocking the wearer unconscious.

Albert Pfisterer, a wiper from the torpedoed *Gulf America*, reported: "We saw bodies in the water, face downwards and feet up. This was the fault of the life preservers. The men could have been saved if it were not for the life preservers crawling up."

The bosun of the *Casper*, which sank in the Baltic Sea years ago, advised that a piece of nine thread line be used to lash the cork preserver around the body to keep it snug and low.

SHIP'S MEETINGS.—John J. Smith, veteran pumpman from the torpedoed Pure Oil tanker *E. W. Hutton*, strongly advocates ship's meetings. Though Smith's ship was torpedoed twice, and men were killed by direct hits, there was an absence of panic among the crew. The discussions aboard the *E. W. Hutton* had much to do in aiding the men, when the emergency came, to keep their heads.

The meetings included the entire crew, divided into two off-watch groups. Besides these meetings, a committee composed of one representative from each department conferred with Captain Carl Flaathan on safety measures.

It was agreed that if no officer were present to take command, the first capable man to reach his lifeboat station, regardless of his rating, was to act as the leader until relieved by a licensed officer. It was also understood that once launched, the lifeboat was to remain nearby until it was certain all survivors had been picked up from the rafts and the water.

The discussions should take place under pleasant circumstances. If dwelling on the subject of abandoning ship causes the men to grow fidgety, discontinue the discussions for a day or two.

TEXTBOOK.—It is suggested that you use this manual, which has been written out of the sweat and blood of actual experience, as the textbook for your meetings. For instance, read Chapter 3 on Buoyancy, and then ask the captain or chief engineer to explain the buoyancy conditions of your own vessel. After this discussion it is likely that you will be able, in an emergency, to put down any impulse to jump into a flaming oil slick or icy water or a shark-infested sea.

DEMONSTRATION.—Thirty-one survivors escaped in a 28-foot lifeboat from the torpedoed *City of New York*. Because of the boat's crowded condition, John Adams, the carpenter, could not get to the mast, and those around it were unable to rig the sail. One adequately trained lifeboatman among 31 persons? The sail had to be passed back to Adams for him to bend on. Then Adams had to shout instructions on how to step the mast.

It is vitally important that the crew—particularly the new seamen, the Black Gang, and those in the steward's department—learn by practice and demonstration the seamanship required in handling a lifeboat. The proper distribution of weight in the lifeboat should be demonstrated to emphasize the importance of maintaining a low center of gravity. Everyone not trained in navigation should read Chapter 9 on

Navigation, and practice shaping courses on a Pilot Chart—before the need to do so arises.

ORDINARIES.—It has been the experience of veteran seamen at ship's meetings that the youngsters are inclined to grin. Consequently the old-timers are equally inclined to drop the discussions. Yet a foolish grin does not make a person's life any less precious.

Actually these ship's boys are grinning to cover their embarrassment, to hide their sense of inadequacy. Perhaps some of them are even incapable of comprehending danger before it reaches them. Whatever the reason, the real seamen are not to allow an irresponsible attitude to affect their zeal in passing on the benefits of their experience.

MORALE.—B. A. Baker, the *Prusa's* third mate, advises: "The most important thing for any lifeboatman to do is to school his own mind. Make up your mind not to get excited and stick to it. Don't say you won't be afraid, for you will. When the torpedo explodes you will get a sinking sensation in the pit of your stomach, and your knees may become a bit weak. The best cure for this is action."

SLACKNESS.—When you review the statistics regarding marine disasters, it is difficult to understand how there ever could be any slackness in lifeboat drills. Yet many a seaman can tell of attending hundreds of drills without once having a chance to lower away and handle a waterborne boat.

Arthur LaBarge, an oiler aboard the *Oneida*, reported on a North Atlantic trip in March: "No lifeboat drills during the entire voyage, going or coming."

Even in peacetime an average of 1,100 oceangoing ships are lost each year. But in wartime Great Britain alone lost three ships a day during 1917, and 2,479 British merchant vessels went down during the first World War. During April 1917, the number of Allied and neutral ships which were sunk totaled 430. The first two weeks of World War II saw 27 British merchant ships go under. In 1917 sixteen British merchant ships were sunk in a single day. Arnauld, a German U-boat commander, using one 4-inch gun—no torpedoes—sank, during three weeks of August 1917, 50 seagoing vessels.

Chapter 2
Abandon Ship

Do NOT RUSH. Sudden sinkings have been rare. But casualties brought about by panicked men dashing needlessly into peril have been frequent.

Fourteen men were saved out of the torpedoed *Naco's* crew of 42. Walter Swank reported: "The men who kept cool and used their heads were those who managed to be saved."

If Ernest Cartwright, one of the three survivors of a freighter shelled more than fifty times, had rushed to get into the port lifeboat, he would have lived less than two minutes. Before they could reach the water, the men in that boat were killed by shellfire.

With no alternative, Cartwright dived overboard. In the waterborne starboard lifeboat he found six more shipmates, four of them dead. These men had *rushed* to their deaths. They had been unable to pause long enough to choose the lesser risk, which was to remain aboard. The freighter itself did not sink for two hours—long after the U-boat had ceased firing.

The chief mate of a torpedoed Panamanian freighter, Hawkins Fudske, entered a lifeboat too soon and was killed by an exploding shell. Yet the men were able to reboard their ship the next day and take her into Mobile, Alabama.

Captain Frank C. Girardeau and all but nine of his men were able to reboard their abandoned ship, after a night spent in the lifeboats, and have her towed into port.

SUCTION.—A slowly sinking vessel may submerge without creating a suction. Vincent Halliburton, from the torpedoed *Ceiba,* reported: "While standing on the boat deck, I felt the ship disappear from under my feet. I started to swim and I picked up a raft."

Few men caught within the suction area of a swiftly sinking ship, except those wearing life suits, have survived.

Hans Sundby, carpenter from the torpedoed Norwegian freighter *Erviken*, reported: "I had the guy to the davit across my shoulders and this prevented me from swimming and caused me to follow the vessel downwards. When I got so far down that I found a terrific pressure against my head, especially the ears, I got free from the wire. I shot up with tremendous power. The suit saved my life by bringing me so quickly to the surface on account of the air trapped inside it."

MAN OVERBOARD.—Do not jump into the water. Unless, like Ernest Cartwright, you have no alternative, or you have to do so to reach a liferaft. If you are wearing a lifejacket containing cork, you are in danger of breaking a rib or your collar bone.

A seaman jumped overboard from the freighter on which Fudske lost his life and was killed by a shark, though the vessel reached port with forty-two men.

FIDLEY   GRATING.—A   man   aboard   the   torpedoed *Collamer,* on watch below, lost his life because of a permanent grating on the fidley skylight.

ENGINE ROOM LADDERS.—Rudolph C. Wellman, second assistant, suggested: "Rope ladders should be hung in the engine room and fireroom so that men will know their location and be able to escape if the regular ladders are blown away."

EMERGENCY ESCAPES.—Thoroughly acquaint yourself with the emergency escapes. Four men on the *Prusa* were lost because they forgot about the emergency escape through the steering engine room. A steam line was severed in the regular passage, making it impossible to leave that way. Yet these men, who were seen in the quarters alive, and apparently uninjured after the explosion, had only to go through the steering engine room up through a manhole onto the poop deck, as two other men did.

BRATTICE CLOTH.—For years brattice cloth—non-inflammable—has been used by miners to shut off a tunnel in the case of fire or a drift when about to shoot a heading. It is now being purchased for many ships, and is of service in partitioning off open alleyways to prevent the passage of flame.

Discuss the feasibility of making a large wind-sail of brattice cloth to surround the Jacob's ladder leading up from the engine room to the skylight.

LIFE SUIT.—Hans Sundby of the *Erviken* reported: "The engineers at work had made the mistake of having their suits in their cabins instead of the passage to the engine room."

SEAWORTHINESS.—Be sure your lifeboat is seaworthy. This may seem like needless advice. Yet in the past bottoms have come out of many lifeboats. One lifeboat of a United Nations freighter, torpedoed 200 miles from Bermuda, leaked so badly that for eleven days the men were unable to stop bailing.

EQUIPMENT.—Do not take it for granted that all the equipment required by law is in your lifeboat. Norman Leo Sampson, the third assistant of a torpedoed freighter, reported that nine of his shipmates were trapped in a lifeboat with no oars. The boat drifted into a sea of blazing oil.

WHISTLE.—Every man should have a whistle made fast around his neck, so that if he is in the water, he can blow the whistle to draw attention.

A severely burned British seaman from a torpedoed gasoline tanker was on the keel of an overturned lifeboat for five days. He was washed off five times, chiefly at night. Since he had a whistle, his shipmates were able to locate him; otherwise he would have been lost.

LIFE LIGHT.—Life lights are manufactured for both jackets and life rings. With good visibility these lights will provide a possibility of attracting rescuers within a radius of at least four miles. Within the visibility range of shore, they offer a three-way chance of drawing attention—from land, sea, and air.

ABANDON-SHIP PACKAGE.—If you are on watch, you should have your life suit, extra clothes, and abandon-ship package with you, so you will not have to lose time returning to your quarters.

WIRE BASKET.—Have the ship's wire baskets or stretchers easily accessible, so that injured persons may be lowered to a waterborne lifeboat. A wire basket may save a simple break from becoming a compound fracture, with its resultant gangrene and possible death.

PAPERS.—After signing the ship's articles, place your papers and valuables in a deposit box ashore. This will relieve your mind of any concern for their safety.

The officers should leave their licenses remaining in the frames aboard ship.

CLOTHES.—Do not sleep undressed. Vincent Santiago, A.B. aboard the *Leslie,* slept almost the entire trip with his clothes on. The first night he took his clothes off, the *Leslie* was torpedoed. For three months McPherson, second mate of the *Exminster,* wore his clothes to bed. The first night he donned pajamas, the *Exminster* was torpedoed.

Even in the tropics have cold-weather clothes in your abandon-ship package, or ready to put on without delay. During five hours of drifting, eleven men clinging to liferafts from the stricken U.S. destroyer *Jacob Jones* succumbed to the cold and slipped into the sea. Yet George Pantall and Thomas Ryan Moody survived. They each had the judgment to don three extra suits of heavy winter underwear.

When a tanker, of which Captain Theron P. Davenport was the master, was torpedoed off the coast of Georgia early in April, the crew had ample time to gather their gear before abandoning ship. Yet most of the men neglected to take along sufficient clothing. Consequently, during the ten hours they were adrift, many of them were severely and needlessly sunburned.

OILSKINS.—Two men, at least, should bring along oilskins. They will be of vital use to the men on watch.

EXTRA FOOD.—You should provide a means to open the potato locker quickly. Get a sack of potatoes in your life-boat, and a sack of onions, if possible, or turnips. Because of their high water content, these vegetables will serve a double purpose in your rations. Canned tomatoes are important. Do not pass up the bottles of jam. The sugar in them will provide energy.

Emergency provisions should be stored in many small watertight containers rather than in one large one. This will lessen the chance of losing your supplies through a container being punctured by shot and the contents being destroyed by salt water.

OTHER EQUIPMENT.—
Jackknife. Do not neglect to take along a knife.

Flashlight. If you have a flashlight and batteries, take them with you. The *Robin Moor's* boat had four torches, in addition to the one required by law.

Rosendo Ramos, from the torpedoed *Republic,* reported: "If each man had a flashlight for use after the lights went out, he could probably have found other ways of escape after the ladder was broken."

Mason Jar. A Mason jar will keep your matches and other small items dry.

Toilet Paper. Take a roll with you.

Flare Pistol. Be sure your lifeboat is equipped with a flare pistol.

Rockets. If time permits, get two or three of the rockets which are stowed on the bridge.

PLUG.—So no one will have difficulty finding the plug, mark it—PLUG. Paint an arrow in white pointing to it.

GREENWICH TIME.—If possible, set your watch to Greenwich time. The mate in your boat may not have a chance to set his watch. He will not be able to calculate longitude with any accuracy without Greenwich time when taking sights.

ORDERS.—Get your orders from the mate. But if you are on your own, be sure to get one boat into the water. That can take care of a freighter's whole crew.

PANIC.—Night puts an added burden on you and you must take extra precautions, because at night there is sure to be more panic than in the daytime.

TIME.—The experience of B.A. Baker, the *Prusa's* third mate, will give you a gauge by which you can judge your own time in an emergency. After she was torpedoed, the *Prusa* sank in exactly nine minutes.

Baker was asleep when the torpedo hit. He went to the bridge and got his sextant, chronometer, and navigation books. He stowed them in the boat and helped lower the boat. Then he went back and tried to get the radio operator to leave. Returning to his room, he obtained a sweater, and then jumped overboard. He swam about 200 feet to the lifeboat. The *Prusa* sank as he was being pulled into the boat.

Chapter 3

Buoyancy

Do NOT JUMP overboard unless you have no alternative. That is what this explanation of buoyancy—the power to keep afloat—is intended to impress upon you.

For a vessel to stay afloat, the upward pressure of the water must be equal to the downward pressure or weight of the vessel. However, because a ship is torpedoed, it does not necessarily follow that the balance of opposing pressures is going to be so altered that the ship must sink. Four men on the torpedoed tanker *Malay* were unable to consider this, and they lost their lives, though the *Malay* itself made port safely.

A vessel is composed of several units. Each hold, as well as the fireroom and engine room, is an *independent* buoyant section.

Picture in your mind a small freight vessel. Visualize each hold as being detached from the other. Each, as you picture it, is now floating independently. The engine room and fireroom, you will see, are floating deep. The #1 and #4 holds are not quite so deep. The #3 hold has less draft, while the #2 hold has the least depth of all.

The sums of all these individual buoyancies make the total buoyancy of the vessel.

Though the tanker *E.H. Blum* was broken in two by a torpedo, the forward half still had sufficient buoyancy to permit it to be towed to port.

Captain Theodore Bockhoff understood the buoyancy set-up of his stricken freighter after it was hit by a torpedo. That is why he ordered Seaman James Sherlock, who was running for the starboard boat, to wait. A few moments later, as the starboard lifeboat reached the water with six men in it, a second torpedo blew it to bits.

When the torpedoed tanker *Gulftrade* broke in two, nine men were on the stern. Seaman Leonard Smith wanted to jump overboard. Guy F. Chadwick, the chief engineer, reminded Smith that the water was cold. "Let's stick with the ship," Chadwick advised, "as long as she'll stick with us." At the very least, the chief's understanding of buoyancy spared a man from exposure and frostbite.

Suppose the vessel is loaded with lumber, and a hold is stove in. Since the specific gravity of wood runs from one-fifth to a slight fraction beyond that of water, the only loss is in the reserve buoyancy, as the lumber's buoyant qualities will substitute for the loss of actual buoyancy. The space which the sea can occupy is only the area not already taken up by the lumber.

Often, when only one or two buoyant sections are immediately damaged, the vessel *eventually* sinks. The *China Arrow*, torpedoed twice, took an hour to sink. This was probably due to the fact that while the destruction of tanks in the vicinity of the blasts was not enough to sink the *China Arrow*, the detonations sheared plates and loosened rivets in the tanks beyond. Buoyancy is often lost on tankers when heat from the oil blaze buckles the plates. Our point is that it takes time for this buoyancy to be lost.

This is borne out by the Latvian freighter *Ciltvaira*. After abandoning ship the men were able to go back, run up SOS flags, and salvage valuables. Captain T.R. Hennevig returned to his crippled freighter eight hours after it had been torpedoed and shelled. A sugar transport vessel, torpedoed off Nuevitas, Cuba, remained afloat and was beached, though 22 crewmen died when lifeboats were sunk by gunfire.

A hold stowed with general cargo presents a serious condition. All the buoyancy of that hold would be lost. Grain cargo likewise adds a threat to a stricken vessel. Expanding from absorbed water, the grain will exert pressure on the watertight bulkhead and loosen rivets.

In short, experience and the laws of physics indicate that men usually have more time to abandon ship than they allow themselves. However, statistics are often contradicted by an individual situation, so don't let them lull you into carelessness. Ships have sunk in five minutes or less.

For your protection, discuss with the mates and engineers the buoyancy problems of your ship. And before you jump, remember that Bryan Lloyd, a seaman, had time to swim back to his ship from a swamped lifeboat, rest five minutes, and release a liferaft. Captain Knut O. Bringedal was able to return to his torpedoed vessel three times. And the tanker *Esso Bolivar,* with water ballast, was towed into port with a 40-foot hole.

Chapter 4

Swinging Out

SWINGING OUT IS a simple process on all types of davits. Even so, a seaman should never attempt something he knows nothing about.

BOAT COVER.—When you remove the boat cover, do not discard it or the spreaders. To get the most use out of the cover in the lifeboat, #7 canvas should be used. The cover should not be painted. Use canvas preserver, which will leave the cover pliable.

STRONGBACK.—Unless you need the strongback as a skate on the high side, throw it overboard.

PAINTER.—Lead the painter well forward, outside of everything. Take up all the slack and make fast properly.

RUDDER.—It is advisable to ship the rudder before the boat is waterborne, but take care that lines are not fouled on it.

PLUG.—Be sure the plug is in.

OUTBOARD GRIPES.—The men are inclined to be afraid to release the outboard gripes. Since a lifebelt will hinder you, it is better not to wear it while you are outboard.

STATIONS.—When they see another boat already swung out, some of the men are liable to leave their stations.

QUADRANTAL DAVITS.—Be sure the pins are in the handles so that the handles will not come off when the men begin cranking outboard.

GRAVITY DAVITS.—With gravity davits one man is able to turn out and lower a lifeboat simply by raising the lever slowly. As the boat rolls down the runway, it should be controlled by frapping lines.

RADIAL DAVITS.—Release the outboard gripes first, then the inboard gripes. Hoist the boat clear of the chocks. Be sure the falls are in the fairleads and belayed on the cleats. Lower the chocks on the deck.

If the boat is to go out bow first, be sure there is clearance aft. Have two men haul on the after guy as the fore guy is being slacked, and the men at the gunwale walk the boat aft.

When the forward davit points directly aft, shove the boat forward and bear out. Slack the after guy and tighten the fore guy.

When the after davit points forward, have the men shove the quarter outboard. Haul on the after guy, square the boat, and make the guys fast.

HIGH SIDE.—Be sure the boat is secured so it will not go athwartship when the gripes are slipped. After the gripes were released on two high-side boats of the *Vestris*—30 degree list—they slid across the deck and rolled overboard.

LOW SIDE.—Be sure you have frapping lines around the falls before you release the boat from the chocks. Otherwise, if the ship has much of a list, the boat will swing out with tremendous force and remain hanging beyond your reach.

Swing the davits out just enough for the boat to clear the ship's side. Do not let go of the handles of the davits until lashings are put on them. As an additional precaution, put wedges in the gears of the davits.

SWUNG OUT.—Remove the boat cover, make it up snugly, and place it in the boat's bottom.

Remove the outboard and inboard gripes.

Lead the sea painter, toggled at the thwart, from the inboard side of the boat well forward, outside of everything.

Do not put the plug in while the boat is hung.

Hoist the boat clear of the chocks until the falls are not quite two-blocked, and swing out. This will two-block the falls.

Fit a stout spar or a strongback to the davits temporarily, so that it may be shifted if necessary.

Chafing pads of good size are fitted to the strongback, so that they are between it and the boat. Shift them to conform with the boat's shape.

Use a handy-billy to haul the boat to the strongback, meanwhile easing the falls gently until snug up.

Keep shifting the strongback and the chafing pads or ease the falls until the boat takes up a satisfactory position.

The boat should then be griped in and the handy-billy removed. The gripes should be fitted with a toggle, if they are not already fitted with pelican or slip hooks.

The slack on the gripes should be taken up from time to time. Thus swung out and griped, the boats require watch-to-watch inspection, especially during heavy weather.

HALF CHOCK.—A safer method of securing the boat ready for quick lowering is to have the boat resting on a half chock, the inboard side. Remove the outboard gripes and lower the outboard half of the chocks. When ready to swing out, trip the releasing gear on the chock and let go the inboard gripes.

Chapter 5

Lowering

THE MAIN CONSIDERATION in lowering is to make certain that at least one boat—which can hold the average merchant ship's entire crew—reaches the water safely. If you see that a shortage of adequately trained seamen is liable to result in swamped boats, take the most competent men from the other boat crews to lower away.

WAY.—It is dangerous for inexperienced seamen to launch a lifeboat where there is way on, though old-timers prefer to have the vessel going ahead. William Caves, for instance, likes to lower when the ship is traveling at about five knots—but Caves is a highly-skilled veteran.

In the last war, 339 men were lost on the torpedoed *Persia*. Because the ship was going ahead, the boats were swamped, torn away, or capsized. On the torpedoed *Maloja* 124 were lost; the ship had sternway. Because the torpedoed *California* had way on, a boat was overturned; 43 lost. The *Antony* was under way when the boats were lowered. The boats were swamped; 55 lost. The engines could not be stopped aboard the *Abosso*. Thirteen lifeboats were swamped; 65 men lost. Way on the *Garmoyle* caused one boat to capsize; 20 lost.

STORM OIL.—If the sea is rough, open the cocks on the storm oil tanks forward.

SKATES.—If the lifeboat is not equipped with skates, use the strongback and oars as skates to get the boat over rims, ports, gangway fittings, and other projections, and past the promenade deck on the high side. In this manner *Vestris* seamen forced a boat down a 30-degree list, launching it successfully.

STERN FAST.—If the ship is pitching, you will need a stern fast as well as a painter, both hauled taut, to keep the boat from swaying.

ORDERS.—If other boats are being lowered, be sure you do not execute an order meant for another boat.

DECK CARGO.—When deck cargo has been washed over the lee side, and is alongside the ship so that it is impossible to launch a lifeboat safely, then a chance has to be taken to lower from the weather side—unless the ship has maneuverability and can be turned around.

FRAPPING LINE.—Frapping lines will keep the boat from swinging. Use one for each fall. On a cargo or tank vessel secure the frapping line to the moving block, or take a bight around the fall. If the line is equipped with a hook, secure the hook on the swivel of the moving block. Handle the frapping lines from the boat deck, a man to each line.

PAYING OUT.—Pay out the fall from a sitting position. That will eliminate the chance of slipping on an ice-covered deck or being overbalanced by a rolling ship.

Wear gloves to avoid rope burns.

See that the falls are properly turned on the cleats.

Lower slowly at first, with sufficient turns so you can pay out smoothly. Avoid jerks, which can exert dangerous strains on the davits, falls, and boats.

Unless you are experienced, do not take your eyes off the bollard or cleat.

Be careful that the fall does not jump off the fairlead. It will let the boat down with a jolt.

The after end of the boat should be slightly lower than the forward end.

JACOB'S LADDER.—The Jacob's ladder should be put over the side amidship of the boat and not alongside a davit.

RELEASING GEAR.—Work the releasing gear about a foot or two above the water. If the releasing gear is operated after the boat is waterborne, it liable to jam.

If the ship has slight way, by handling the rudder you can steer the boat away from the ship's side. This eliminates the danger of another boat being dropped on the waterborne one.

Operate the releasing gear when the ship has reached the limit of its downward roll.

Release the boat as a sea approaches, so that the boat will drop on the crest.

Chapter 6

Waterborne

ONCE YOUR HIGHLY buoyant lifeboat is waterborne, no difficult process is required to keep it from capsizing. You merely
must have the weight distributed properly. Allow no one to
stand on a thwart. Five men can do all that is necessary to get
the boat away from the ship's side. In a heavy sea maintain a
low center of gravity by having the balance of the crew keep
down on the bottom boards.

BLOCKS.—As soon as the releasing gear is operated, watch
out for swinging blocks.

FALLS.—Falls may be used to slide down in abandoning ship.

BOAT HOOK.—Have a man shove off from the ship's side with a boat hook or oar.

PAINTER.—Have the bow man haul as much of the painter into the boat as possible before he cuts loose. This will give you extra line. Pulling up on the rope will put the boat in motion, enabling the man at the tiller to steer, providing the sea is not too rough.

OAR LASHINGS.—When letting go the lashings on the oars, be sure only half of them are turned loose. Otherwise, if the boat capsizes, all the oars will be lost.

OARSMEN.—It is not necessary to man all of the oars. One oarsman on each side will be able to get the boat away from the ship quickly. They should row immediately at right angles to the ship to eliminate the possibility of another boat being lowered on top of the waterborne one.

ROWING.—It is difficult to row in a heavy sea. The men can last at it about fifteen minutes, and by making every stroke count, can perhaps get a half mile from the ship.

Be sure you do not start pulling on the oar before it is in the water.

Keep your eye on the stroke oar on each side of the boat.

Put the weight of your body on the oar. In a boat properly rowed a thrumming noise issues from the oars and gives a sense of timing.

In a double-banked boat be careful that you do not draw a longer stroke than the man in front of you. If you do, you are liable to dig him in the back with the handle of your oar.

FEATHERING.—While it is the customary practice to grasp the handle of the oar with both hands on the upper side, many oarsmen find it easier to feather with one hand on the upper side and one hand on the under side. This is the grip used by Negro seamen of the West Indies. They are exceptional oarsmen. The grip is also used by the Ellis and Gilbert Islanders, and no finer oarsmen live.

Do not feather until the blade is clear of the water. If you do so, the oar will be forced down by the way of the boat and it will likely foul the oar behind you.

At this time feathering is not important. Your chief concern should be to get clear of the ship's suction area.

LIFE PRESERVER.—If everything is behaving properly, and the men realize the importance of keeping the weight distributed evenly, there is no need to continue wearing your life preserver. Drop it to the bottom of the boat.

SEA ANCHOR.—Put out the sea anchor and rest up. Do not attempt to set sail immediately. Wait until shock, confusion, and panic have subsided. When the panicked crew of the torpedoed Norwegian freighter *Blink* tried to hoist a sail, the lifeboat capsized, throwing 23 men into icy water and immediately costing one man's life. Food, water, oars, and sail were lost.

MAN OVERBOARD.—Be sure no one is near a churning propeller. Herbert L. Gardner, Jr., wiper from an Atlantic Refining Co. tanker, saw two shipmates caught in the propeller's suction and dragged into the blades to their death.

Men have died by being struck by rescue boats. Approach a man in the water no closer than the distance needed to reach him with an outstretched oar.

PISTOL.—Be sure that no hot-headed shipmate has a gun. Firing it at the sub will only draw fire on your boat. Besides, it is unlawful for merchant seamen to possess firearms.

PANIC.—Away from the ship in a lifeboat that is riding nicely, you have little or no cause for panic. When the *Robin Moor* men heard machine-gun fire, they were stricken with terror that they would be shot. But the sub's gunners were merely indulging in target practice, firing at wreckage.

If the enemy intended to machine-gun a crew, they generally would not let the crew get off the ship.

The sub commander who sank the *Robin Moor* provided extra rations for the crew and first-aid materials for Chief Officer Mundy. P. H. Janssen, fireman from a torpedoed American freighter, after being hauled aboard a submarine by the German crew, spent five minutes on its deck before he was transferred to a lifeboat.

More likely than not, you will find that enemy sailors will give you the same treatment they would expect to receive.

BULLET HOLE.—Do not give up because a hole is shot in your boat. The airtanks will float her, and with proper tools any boat can be patched at sea.

In a sheet-metal boat, if you have sheet-metal screws, a prick punch and a screwdriver, by cutting up an airtank you can patch in an hour a hole one foot in diameter.

Chapter 7

Setting Sail

SHIP'S DISCIPLINE MUST not be relaxed in the lifeboat. There is much work that has to be done; and the sooner the men are apportioned their duties, the better it will be for their morale.

SETTING SAIL.—Before you step the mast, reeve the halyard through the sheave. Step the mast and tighten up on the stays. Bend the halyard about one-third of the way up on the yard-arm, starting from the fore leech. The fore leech is easily recognizable because it is shorter than the after leech, or after end, of the sail.

No downhaul is required. Bend the tack to the stem or cross bows, depending on whether the wind is abeam or on the quarter, for your proposed track. Hoist the sail. Then tighten up on the halyard. Secure it at the foot of the mast, or use it as a stay. Haul in the sheet until the sail fills.

SETTING WATCHES.—Set the watches the same as aboard ship, one man in charge of a watch, the best men for the late parts of the night. Once a man learns what to do, he is expected to show initiative. He should know enough to change course when the wind changes, and to inform the mate of it when the latter wakes up.

RATIONING FOOD.—Put a responsible person in charge of the rations.

If you have potatoes and onions in the extra rations, keep them dry or they will sprout. If they take up too much space, remove them from the sacks and drop them along the side benches on top of the tanks.

On dry days inspect the food to see if anything is spoiled and to find out what is on hand.

If rations are short, the men must conserve their energy, moving about only enough to keep the kinks out of their knees. And watch out for the kinks—in case you have to move fast in a squall.

RATIONING WATER.—Be sure you know, before the emergency arises, the amount of fresh water in your lifeboat. The seven men in a boat from the torpedoed British freighter *Anglo-Saxon* found only four gallons in their breaker. Five of those men never reached land.

Use this simple method to determine how long your supply will last:

Your water breaker contains, we will say, 15 gallons—128 ounces to the gallon—or 1920 ounces. Dividing by 6 ounces—the average ration—you learn that the breaker contains 320 cups of water. Subtract 20 cups, because the breaker is not entirely full—to allow for expansion during the winter months—and you have 300 cups of 6 ounces.

This amount will provide water 3 times a day for 100 days.

(100 ÷ Number in boat) equals number of days the water will last.

RAIN WATER.—For rain water use an airtank from the stern—never one of the forward or waist tanks. Because in heavy weather the boat will ship water frequently in these sections, there is a greater need of the airtanks to maintain buoyancy.

In collecting water, you will find that it takes a lot of rain to get the salt out of the sail. Therefore, you should have an extra piece of canvas to be used only for catching water, or better still, a piece of oiled silk or even oilcloth.

You are advised against using the boat cover to collect water. Not only is it soaked with salt, but if the boat cover has been treated with canvas preserver, the water will become foul in warm weather.

Stop for water during heavy squalls. If the squalls are frequent, you need to stop only long enough to make up for what has been drunk during the day.

Care must be used in storing an airtank full of water, so as not to upset the boat's stability, or put an undue stress on the bottom.

COMPASS.—Use the staples from the lifelines to secure the compass aft for the man at the tiller. Lubber's line should line up with the center of the keel.

If the alcohol is missing from the compass, fresh water may be substituted, though it will corrode the metal. As a last resort in freezing weather, fill your compass with water, wrap it well, or bank it with snow, and keep the compass light burning.

FLARES.—When you have occasion to use one, lash a flare to the end of an oar, so the men will not be blinded by its glare. Be sure to keep it away from the sail.

SEA ANCHOR.—To make a sea anchor: With a hatchet cut two metal rings, about one-inch wide, from the tank used for rain water. Cut the rings to break the circle, and pull each one out to form a half-circle. Split one end of each half-circle by making two cuts, and fit them together so as to make one large ring or grommet. Hammer the joints tight and secure with marlin. Serve the grommet with rope yarn or marlin, so it will not cut through the canvas.

Set the canvas up in a conical shape and sew the ring to it. Add bridles and line. You will have a sea anchor that is similar to those ordinarily found in lifeboats.

In case no canvas is available for a sea anchor, secure a bucket or a can in the center of an oar. Secure a line to each end of the oar and make the lines fast, one to each side of the boat, well forward.

OARS.—Lash all the oars, not otherwise in use, on the weather side. This will raise the lee side, and will help to prevent swamping.

STEERING OAR.—If you use the steering oar, fasten a short lanyard on it near the leather—the part of the oar which rests in the oar lock. That will eliminate the chance of losing it. The lanyard also allows you to walk away from the oar. In rough weather, kneel with the steering oar; do not stand.

RAIL.—To build a rail, lash an oar to the mast, and fit one end in the crotch of a boat hook which has been secured upright. Cut the staff of the boat hook to make a stanchion of sufficient height. Use adequate lashings. The rail will aid the men going forward or aft. By standing on a thwart, supported by others and resting against the rail, the mate will be better able to take a sight.

MAST.—Many times in stepping a mast, the tenon on the heel of the mast proves to be too small for the mortise of the step, in which case you will have to wedge the tenon to fit tightly.

SPREADERS.—You can use the spreaders to make tillers, or you can cut them up for use as wedges.

BOAT COVER.—The boat cover will shelter you from the sun and rain. A piece of it can be used to increase the sail area. Use other pieces to keep dry the sextant and chronometer, which may be stowed aft in the space of the airtank that you are using for rain water. The cover lashings, as well as the grab lines, will supply extra line for replacements and additions to stays and halyards.

SAIL BAG.—By slitting the sail bag at the seams, you will have extra canvas for increasing the sail area.

Chapter 8
Open Boat Seamanship

THE IMPORTANT FACT to remember about sailing is that the average double-end lifeboat, in good condition, is exceptionally seaworthy. It is far better equipped to fight a storm than you are. In any kind of a gale, do not try to sail the lifeboat. You will only be offering resistance against a greater force, thus inviting disaster without getting anywhere. But if the men keep down on the bottom boards, creating a low center of gravity, the boat will be able to take a terrific pounding without capsizing.

REEF.—In hoisting sail in a stiff breeze, always reef your sail first. If it is not needed, the reef can easily be shaken out.

TILLER.—When you move the tiller to port, the boat turns to starboard, and vice versa.

In good weather handling the tiller is child's play. It is then that you should pick up pointers and gain confidence in steering.

SAILING.—To get the best results in speed, the sail should be kept as nearly as possible at right angles.

A boat rigged with a dipping lug sail cannot point higher than 8 points to the wind—which means a beam wind— and make any speed. To reduce somewhat the considerable amount of leeway—the sideways drift caused by the pressure of the wind—which a beam wind causes, shift as much weight as you can to the weather side.

FOLLOWING SEA.—You should learn to steer in a following sea during the daytime.

Keep a following sea on your quarter.

Caution: When a following sea starts to break on you, do not pull the tiller away from the sea. If you do, you will bring the boat broadside toward the oncoming sea—with the danger of being swamped.

In a following sea, always put the tiller toward the breaking sea. Hold it there while the sea is rushing upon you, bringing the tiller amidship when the sea has passed. You must repeat this maneuver again and again—every time the sea is about to break.

At night, when the water is phosphorescent, it is easy to determine which way the sea is breaking.

It is much easier to steer at night as well as by day if a white pennant is hoisted on a boat hook just forward of the helmsman to show the direction of the wind.

COMPASS.—It is not necessary to watch the compass. It gives you only a general direction. *Watch the sail.* If you are making good speed, do not worry about keeping a course.

SQUALLS.—In squally weather you will be able to make excellent speed; but the boat will be very lively, and much care will be required in handling it and the sail. In heavy squalls shorten the sail by reefing and be alert for a sudden shift of wind—or the sail may be caught aback, that is, reversed.

WIND.—When running before the wind, it is always best to have the wind on your quarter in preference to astern. With the wind on your quarter, you will get the most speed out of the boat.

If the wind veers, it is going clockwise. To keep the veering wind on the quarter, put the helm up to it.

If a sharp puff of wind hits the boat, ease the helm.

SEA ANCHOR.—Used as a drag, the sea anchor will keep the boat in line with the wind and the sea.

Great care must be taken in using the sea anchor as a drag. Watch out that the line does not unlay, kink up, and break apart, all of which can happen within a very few minutes.

When riding out a gale, the sea anchor should be over the bow.

When their sea anchor was lost, the *Robin Moor* men used the oars to keep the boat head on. The boat took such a pounding that the men let it go broadside to. With the weight low, the boat rode nicely. In a very rough sea, you must not attempt this. With water towering around the boat, there will be too much risk of it filling up and swamping. In a rough sea, keep the boat head on. If the sea anchor has been lost, use the oars.

LEE SIDE.—Since the men are used to walking on the lee side aboard ship, they must be cautioned *not* to walk on the lee side of the lifeboat. Their weight on the lee side is liable to capsize the boat. The men must keep on the weather side, and as close to aft as possible, to hold the rudder down in the water.

SHEET.—Do not make the sheet fast. If an incompetent man is on watch, and a heavy blow comes up, there is a grave danger of the boat capsizing. You may take a turn around a cleat, but be sure that you can let go the sheet instantly.

Never haul the sheet so tight that the foot of the sail is inside the gunwale.

COLLISION.—When the boats are together, the men are apt to become a bit playful, especially at night if the mates are asleep. Care must be taken that the men do not run the boats too close and have a collision.

STORM OIL.—To help prevent seas from breaking, use storm oil. All lifeboats are provided by law with storm oil. A conical-shaped can is inserted in the sea anchor. By cracking the tap sufficient oil will flow to make a slick.

LAGOON GLARE.—Near lagoon islands in the South Pacific, a lagoon glare will be visible on clear days. This is a light greenish tint in the sky caused by the reflection of the sun from the coral on the bottom of the lagoon. It is often very pronounced, and is sometimes visible up to 75 miles. With only a compass, Baker, the *Prusa's* third mate, has navigated a small boat between the islands in the Gilberts by this glare.

CLOUDS.—A cumulus cloud over water, when the sky is relatively clear, usually indicates an island. If only one cloud is in the sky, and it is cumulus—which has the appearance of heaped, rounded masses—an island is practically assured.

COAST GUARD SIGNALS.—

"Do not attempt to land in your own boats."

Day: Red flag, white flag, waved together.
Night: Red lantern, white lantern, waved together.

"This is the best place to land."

Day: A man beckoning on the beach.
Night: Two torches burning together on the beach.

LANDING.—Near land is where impatience too often has cost lives. If the breakers are heavy, wait outside, if possible, until they moderate.

Do not leave your lifeboat and attempt to swim through surf in a rough sea, unless it is your only choice.

As you approach the beach in the boat, look for the spot where the breakers are the least heavy. Head straight for the beach. The sea anchor must be over the stern. The oarsmen must keep a strain on the drag line. That strain will prevent the sea from throwing the stern around and capsizing the boat. Use oil to help keep the seas from breaking.

Coming to the beach, as the boat reaches the crest of the last sea, the oarsmen should pull strenuously. The farther you can get the boat up on the beach, the less chance there will be of capsizing.

Your greatest danger is when the bow becomes buried in a sea. This is one reason why you must never remove the air tanks.

A good method of rowing through surf is to have half of the crew sit in the opposite direction to the others. When a heavy sea roars down, have one-half of the crew row toward the sea until the crest passes. Then have the other half row toward the shore until the next sea comes along. Remember that in surf landings the seas are irregular and their velocities varied.

When the gunboat *Tacoma* went aground on Blanquilla Reef near Vera Cruz in 1924, William Caves used this method in taking a line to the reef for a breeches buoy. With six men, three sitting each way, Caves was able to get a 13-foot dinghy through heavy surf.

Chapter 9
Navigating

IF YOUR LIFEBOAT is without a navigator, these directions are for you. There is nothing difficult about them. They are as simple as the directions for a child's game. But they will provide you with the key to your own rescue.

Before leaving your home port, purchase a U.S. Hydrographic Office "Pilot Chart" covering the area of your ship's route. Pilot Charts cost ten cents a sheet, and are obtainable at any nautical store. If you are a soldier or sailor, and consequently do not know your route or destination, we suggest that you buy for sixty cents the six sections taking in the entire world.

Disregard the printed statement that the chart is not to be used for navigation. For your purposes it is entirely adequate. During the nineteen days in the *Robin Moor* lifeboat, Banigan daily plotted his position on a Pilot Chart.

If you have no chart, and do not know of any islands North or South of you, set your course as close to due East or due West as the winds will permit, and eventually you will sight land.

With a Pilot Chart and knowledge of your approximate position, you can plot the track or route you should take, simply by observing the nearest point of land from you.

Whether the average winds are in your favor can be readily seen by the wind roses on the chart along your chosen track. The chart provides adequate instructions regarding the wind roses.

If you are an untrained man, do not concern yourself with the set of the current. Your guess as to allowance will undoubtedly be out of proportion.

Obtain your true course—the one you intend to steer by—in this simple manner:

Note the compass rose—the circle on the chart that is graduated from 0 to 360 degrees.

Take two sticks or pieces of cardboard.

Lay one on the proposed track.

Lay the second stick across the center of the compass rose parallel to the first stick. Use the stick in the same way you would use a ruler.

Read off the course indicated by the stick on the compass rose *in the direction of the proposed track.*

Note the lines of variation plainly indicated as to the amount and direction, East or West.

Variation is the difference between the true or geographical North and the magnetic North.

But don't worry your head about what variation is. Concern yourself merely with what you have to do about it.

Variation represents an error which you must correct.

If it is stated on the Pilot Chart that the variation is *West— add* the amount of variation to the course indicated by the stick on the compass rose. If the variation is *East—subtract*.

The answer is the course to steer.

So long as the sail is kept full, a lifeboat rigged with a dipping lug sail will average between 3 to 4 knots in a moderate breeze. Gauging your speed by this, and mindful of the chart's scale of measurements, you can plot your position day by day.

The scale of latitude is used for measuring distances.

You will find this scale on the right- and left-hand sides of the chart. One degree equals 60 miles or minutes. The scale is graduated in 6 parts of 10 minutes each.

Always measure off distance near your parallel of latitude.

The scale of longitude is graduated in the same way as the scale of latitude. But never use the scale of longitude to measure your distance.

When there is any shift in the wind which may require a change in course, you should make each change, if possible, in the general direction of your proposed track.

We have made no attempt to teach the elements of navigation, but we have presented a working plan which will help you to reach land or the steamer tracks where you have a chance of being picked up.

Chapter 10

Transports

In TRANSPORTING TROOPS the government works on a wide margin of safety. Measures of precaution are heaped upon one another. During the last war, four or five of the larger troopships would be escorted by six or eight destroyers, equal to three times as much protection per ship as was given mercantile convoys.

More than 2,000,000 American soldiers were transported to France without a casualty on the eastbound trip. By June and July of 1918 about 300,000 U.S. troops a month were crossing the Atlantic.

This success was due in part to the fact that the Germans were concentrating on merchant shipping and homebound empties, and made only a few feeble attempts against our troopships. They did sink the U.S. transport *President Lincoln,* but she was a westbound empty, and only 26 persons were lost.

Despite all the measures of safety, U.S. troops were killed on transports. The British *Tuscania* was torpedoed in February 1918, and 213 American soldiers died. The *Otranto* was sunk by collision, and 431 U.S. troops were killed.

The point to remember is that when transports are hit, the loss of life is terrific: *Arcadian,* 279; *Aragon,* 610; *Louvain,* 224; *Santa Anna,* 638; *Leasowe Castle,* 101; *Galway Castle,* 189. These figures should induce a soldier at sea to be at all times vigilant and alert.

He should acquaint himself with every rule and regulation regarding his own safety. He must realize that the restrictions in area and other regulations, absolutely unavoidable in handling the mass, become an added hazard to the individual's safety. He must understand that in abandoning ship his superior officers are governed by orders and regulations, and are not fortified by experience. When a torpedo hits, the government's wide margin for mass protection becomes a narrow margin for individual error.

APPROXIMATE POSITION.—You are to be given the approximate position of the transport at the time of abandoning ship. Without this approximate position you will not be able to set a course for the nearest point of land.

A transport's abandon-ship facilities are based on the probability that the survivors will be picked up within a short while. Since weather or other conditions may prevent your immediate rescue, you should make individual preparations for your safety. Among these individual precautionary measures should be the purchase at any nautical store of six 10¢ Pilot Charts, covering the entire world.

SILENCE.—After the order is given to abandon ship, keep quiet. No one is to talk except those who are giving the orders or supervising the execution of them.

OFFICERS.—Non-commissioned officers are not to leave the transport until all their men have left. Commissioned officers must be the last to leave the ship.

ORDERS.—Do not obey any orders except those given by the officers. Follow these orders out as you were instructed during the drills. Be sure that you do not misinterpret an order. Do not forget that you alone—by not knowing what to do—may be the cause of a panic.

QUARTERS.—Since you will be assigned to a certain section of the ship for the duration of the trip, you must acquaint yourself with the alleyways, companionways, and other means of escape in your area. Be sure you know your alternative if any of these exits are cut off. Use only the alleyways and exits assigned to your unit.

During your recreation period study the details of the ship's construction. Find the places which will afford protection during shellfire or bombing. Be sure you know the most direct route to your raft or boat station.

UNDERCLOTHING.—Said John J. Smith, pumpman from a torpedoed tanker: "From now on, winter or summer, the tropics or the arctic, I'm wearing heavy woolen underwear."

Despite the discomfort, wear heavy underclothing the entire voyage.

RATIONS.—Though your boat or raft will be supplied with rations, it is advisable to take along extra rations. Concentrated food can be carried in a large-sized money belt.

LIFE PRESERVERS.—If your preserve is a cork jacket, obtain a piece of nine thread or stout cord to tie around it. This will keep the preserver snug and low. It will lessen your difficulty in going down a lifeline, and your head will not be forced under water, which is one of the tricks of these treacherous, high-riding jackets.

LIFEBOATS.—Every other boat should be lowered on each side to reduce the possibility of one boat being dropped on another.

LIFERAFTS.—The rafts should be released one after the other on both sides, beginning from the after end of the ship. This will prevent the rafts from bunching up and will allow the men more freedom of movement over a larger area.

LIFELINES.—Do not jump overboard. Your cork jacket will knock you out and cripple you. It may cost your life. Use a line, net, or ladder.

LIST.—The torpedoed transport *Transylvania* was sunk in May 1917, with a loss of 269. A slight list was corrected by massing the troops on the high side, an example of the practical use of moveable weight. Had the men gone over the low side, greater losses would have been incurred.

SHELLFIRE.—Should the enemy, by shellfire or bombs, destroy the boat or raft to which you have been assigned, do not attempt to crowd into another boat or raft. Depend on your lifebelt for the time being.

EXHAUSTION.—Cold and exposure will hasten exhaustion. An exhausted man should be transferred to a lifeboat.

SHOCK.—Have an understanding with the men in your unit to watch one another for signs of shock, which often works by delayed action. Many men have perished in the water who could have been saved with a little assistance during a seizure or relapse.

Chapter 11
Liferafts

LIFERAFTS ARE SO varied in design and capacity that you must find out for yourself the limitations of the raft to which you may have to entrust your life.

PONTOON RAFTS.—The lattice boards on the pontoon rafts are nailed down. When the rafts hit the water, the impact splinters them, and the nails often protrude. Nailed boards even pull apart from the seas hitting them. The boards should be bolted. If this is not done, then a pontoon raft should be eased into the water with a line.

TANKERS.—Tanker rafts should be launched near enough to waterborne lifeboats so that a line can be passed from the boat to the raft. If this is not possible, the raft is to be considered a death trap, and is to be used only as a last resort, or when there is no oil slick.

SCREWS.—The suction area of a revolving screw is thirty feet or more, depending on the r.p.m. Therefore, rafts secured aft must be launched outside of this area. Be sure that the wind and the sea will not cause the raft to drift into the suction area.

RATIONS.—Do not depend on the liferaft being equipped with adequate rations, or on the man detailed to bring along a watertight package of food. Any food in your abandon-ship package that lacks a waterproof covering is certain to be spoiled. It is advisable to equip yourself with a water-repelling money belt to hold concentrated food in airtight containers. A canteen filled with water and strapped to your waist will not hamper you.

PROPULSION.—The prime purpose of a raft is to get you out of the suction area of a sinking ship and to keep you afloat until you can be picked up. Yet Gene Aldrich, Harold Dixon, and Anthony J. Pastula, Navy fliers, spent 34 days in a rubber liferaft, whose inside dimensions were 28 x 80 inches, and traveled 1000 miles chiefly by drifting. But by cutting the uppers from a pair of shoes with thick rubber soles, they made usable paddles.

OARLOCKS.—The men on a liferaft from an Atlantic Refining Co. tanker took turns serving as human oarlocks. Their bodies were badly bruised and their hands severely burned. These injuries could have been avoided by crossing the bights of the grab lines and putting the oars through the loops. They also could have used their leather belts.

WEIGHT.—Be sure the weight is distributed properly on your liferaft. If you are on a decked-over liferaft, do not sit up in a heavy sea or you will be washed overboard. Lie down and grip the lattice-work deck.

TRIP RELEASE.—Paul Voss, A.B. from the torpedoed *Collamer*, reported: "Had liferafts been secured with a trip system other than a pelican hook, the man who releases the raft would not be in danger of being hit by the wire pennant holding the raft in place."

DOUBLE TRIP RELEASE.—The seamen on the *Patrick J. Hurley* suggested: "A double trip release should be provided for each of the liferafts, one operated from the bridge and the other from the liferaft."

KNIFE.—The *Gulftrade* seamen advised that a knife should be attached to each raft.

BLANKETS.—Be sure your raft is supplied with sufficient blankets.

LUBRICANT.—V.B. Hair of the *Cardonia* advised: "Fuel oil should not be put on the runways of liferafts. This dries and is more like glue than a lubricant."

WIRE ROPE.—It is advisable not to lash the rafts with wire rope. On the *Cardonia* a fire ax had to be used to cut the lashings on a raft.

LIFEBOAT.—If there is room in a lifeboat, once you are away from the ship, do not remain on the raft. Four men on a raft from a Norwegian freighter were washed overboard and drowned, though the crewmen in a nearby lifeboat could have transferred them to their boat.

DESTROYER.—If you are on a destroyer, you must get your raft out of the explosion area of depth charges when the destroyer goes under. About 30 men from the *Reuben James* were killed when their rafts, 75 feet from the sunken destroyer, were blown out of the water by depth bombs. Do not be lax because someone tells you that the safety catches on the charges have been locked.

When the *Jacob Jones* went down, she exploded with such lethal force that the nearby rafts were blown out of the water, and a number of the men clinging to them were fatally injured.

LEE SIDE.—Make every effort to maneuver your raft to the lee of the vessel, so the raft will drift away from the sinking ship. Joseph Paul Tidwell, from the *Jacob Jones*, reported that the sea kept driving his three-man raft back toward the destroyer.

SEA ANCHOR.—Harold F. Dixon, the Aviation Chief Machinist's Mate who spent 34 days in a rubber liferaft, said he rigged a sea anchor out of his pneumatic life jacket, bridled to a length of the half-inch Manila grab line and weighted down with the raft's gas-inductor manifold.

RAIN WATER.—If you have no other means of catching rain water, cut strips from your underwear and use them to soak up water.

STOWED RAFTS.—The crew of the *Rubilene* reported: "Our liferafts were lashed to the deck or set in walkways where they served only to bruise shins during blackouts."

Chapter 12
Tankers

WILLIAM CAVES, THE bosun of the torpedoed tanker *Harry F. Sinclair, Jr.*, said that flames from the gasoline spreading over the water were 75 feet high. In view of such a frightening picture, it is difficult to warn you against panic.

Yet the records of torpedoed tankers bear out that, barring a direct hit, panic is your greatest danger. Captains have been forced to report that their men were lost because they would not obey orders. When flames are shooting skyward and the sea is afire, stake your life on a veteran's judgment. Men who have yielded to blind, hysterical impulses have seldom come out alive.

Said Alfred Carini, chief mate of the torpedoed *Pan-Massachusetts:* "I lost everything but my head, and because I kept my head, I did not lose my life."

LIFEBOATS INBOARD.—William Caves advises against having tanker lifeboats already swung out. If the men get to a boat before an officer or bosun, they are liable to launch it into flames.

LIFEBOAT CAPACITY.—It is difficult to maneuver a lifeboat in an oil slick, and particularly so if it is loaded to capacity. If possible, a tanker lifeboat should not carry more than half its complement. Fifteen persons, for instance, would be an ample load for a 28-foot boat.

LOWERING.—Because there is a grave chance that some of the men are not going to reach their stations, every tanker-man must know every boat job.

Be sure enough men are in the boat to handle it when it hits the water. Four are sufficient. The radio operator was alone in the *Harry F. Sinclair's* #2 boat. When it became waterborne, he could not prevent it from drifting into the flames. His charred body was recovered.

LIFELINES.—The lifelines should be lowered before the falls are paid out. Lifelines coiled in a *City of New York* boat fouled on the men in the boat, and four of them were yanked over the side. They lost their lives.

LADDER.—Ladders are constructed to reach the water when the tanker is light. On a loaded tanker the end of the ladder reaches into the water, dragging astern. The ladder should be secured on deck so that this is avoided.

PAINTER.—If you cannot fireproof the painter, use 30 feet of wire, with a Manila tail leading into the boat.

STEERING OAR.—Because of oil slicks, a steering oar is preferable to a rudder in getting away from the ship.

OARLOCK.—A Navy-style steering oarlock should be used. The ordinary type is of little service for a tanker. The steering oar has to be lashed to it, and the lashing is liable to burn.

OVERBOARD DISCHARGE.—If the torpedo has hit within the vicinity of the overboard discharge, any boat launched near the overboard discharge will be in danger of being swamped.

LIFERAFTS.—Because you have no control over them, rafts are useless for tankers, except under the most favorable conditions, and are to be considered as death traps.

RAFT RELEASING GEAR.—As long as the rafts are put on board, they should be given as much utility value as possible. Because a hot deck may prevent you from getting to the raft, you should secure a line to the releasing gear so that the raft may be released from a distance.

RAFT SKIDS.—A steel skid should be built between the mainmast and the break of the poop, at about #8 tank. The ladder should be lowered from the fore part of the poop. The waterborne raft will not collide with the lifeboat, but it will be close enough so that a line can be passed to it from the lifeboat.

Another steel skid should be erected between #2 and #3 tanks. The raft will float back abreast of the bridge, where a ladder should be lowered.

OIL SLICK.—In the thick coating of oil around the torpedoed *E.W. Hutton,* John J. Smith and his crew found it difficult to maneuver their lifeboat. Certainly then, a man who plunges into an oil slick, hindered by a cork jacket, will encounter much greater difficulty in getting clear.

Captain E.V. Peters jumped for a lifeboat as a sea swung the boat away from the hull. He fell into water that was thickly covered with fuel oil.

Christian A. Hansen, the first mate, reported: "Captain Peters was a good swimmer, but you can't swim in that. It paralyzes you. We heard him holler, 'Here I am,' and we yelled, 'We're coming,' but by the time we could row back toward the ship there was no sign of the captain."

L. Leslie Pilbean, a British ship's baker and a veteran of six torpedoings, used a successful method of swimming in an oil slick. When his ship, the *Ulysses,* was torpedoed, he had to swim in an oil slick for two and a half hours. Some of his shipmates were lost because they tried to swim on the surface, which is like attempting to swim through thick mud.

Pilbean survived because he swam under water, came up for air, and went under again, repeating this process until he was rescued.

CORK PRESERVERS.—No man from the *Harry F. Sinclair* who hit the water with a cork jacket got away. Richard

Haigland, the chief mate, was knocked out by his cork life preserver. His charred body was recovered.

Even in going down a rope you will find a cork jacket treacherous.

WIND.—When your boat is waterborne, watch out that the wind does not change. Get to windward of the oil slick or flames as soon as possible.

WET TOWELS.—Captain Robert E. Christy, master of the torpedoed *Pan-Massachusetts,* got safely through the fire that framed his cabin by wrapping heavy wet towels around his head, face, and hands.

MOORING LINE.—Twenty men perished in the flaming sea surrounding the *Pan-Massachusetts,* but Captain Christy with three others were among the survivors. They made fast a mooring line on the fo'c'sle head, lowered the line over the side, waited until the bow was clear of flames, and slid down the line into the water.

TORPEDO FUMES.—The fumes from the torpedo made all of the *E.W. Hutton* men so ill that they vomited. A wet handkerchief, to which has been added a few drops of aromatic spirits of ammonia, tied over your nose and mouth will help prevent this distress.

SWIMMING.—Anderson, an oiler from the *Harry F. Sinclair,* swam under water. From time to time he looked up and saw the flames. He stayed under until he was out of the flame area. Few men could have accomplished this.

A messboy from the same tanker came up, fought the flames back, took a breath, and swam under water again. He was severely burned. A woman's bathing cap, fitting over the ears and fastening under the chin, would have greatly reduced his burns.

Both men agreed that with cork jackets they would not have gotten through.

Other seamen have dived into flames and managed to swim underwater to safety. It is extremely hazardous and is strongly advised against. If a seaman must swim, he should do so to windward.

JUMPING.—If you must jump—as a last resort—wait for a clear spot, gauge the distance, and be sure you are facing to windward.

SHEAF KNIFE.—As soon as the vessel is at sea, sheaf knives should be distributed to tankermen.

Oily hands prevented the *E.W. Hutton* men from opening jackknives.

PUMPMAN.—Every Saturday morning, John J. Smith, the *E.W. Hutton's* pumpman, made it a part of his routine to oil and grease the davits.

TANKS.—The smothering lines should be open at all times, and while ballast is being pumped, all those tanks not being used for ballast should be steamed for about 12 hours.

Live steam entering a tank under pressure is a dynamic gas which by its movement disperses the pockets of oil gas, with the continuing flow of steam forcing the mixture of oil gas and steam out through the open trunk. This action is aided by the heat of the steam, which causes the oil gas to separate into several components, the most readily volatile being driven off first. This steaming will eliminate the danger of an explosion.

LIFE SUIT.—A life suit should be considered an indispensable part of a tankerman's equipment. Each man should either wear the suit while working or sleeping, or else he should have the suit always in a position to be donned in the shortest possible time.

PORTHOLE.—One man in every room must be responsible for the porthole—to see that the deadlight is dogged down at 5 p.m.

FLASHLIGHT.—In every room a dry cell battery light should be hanging on the bulkhead by the door. The room should also be supplied with a flashlight.

STOREROOM.—The storeroom should be unlocked at night.

CIGARETTES.—Since coastwise tankers are not required to carry slop chests, all lifeboats should be supplied with watertight cartons of cigarettes.

RADIO SHACK.—The radio shacks on tankers should be moved aft or an auxiliary set should be installed there. If the tanker is fitted with a mizzen mast, an auxiliary vertical aerial should be rigged.

Chapter 13
Medical

BE SURE YOU include medical supplies in your abandon-ship package. All seamen, and everyone who may have to abandon ship, should carry at all times a waterproof packet containing at least two ounces of sulfanilamide powder.

SULFANILAMIDE.—R.H. Pilcher, the radio operator of the torpedoed *Anglo-Saxon*, had his left foot mangled by shrapnel. His foot turned green and black from gangrene, which is dead tissue. It swelled to twice its natural size. The stench from it made his lifeboat mates sick. On the seventh day the foot went dead, and on the eleventh day the remains of Pilcher were dropped over the side.

Sulfanilamide, the miracle drug, even administered by unskillful hands, undoubtedly would have saved Pilcher's life.

In the First World War 80% of the men suffering from abdominal wounds were killed by infection. After Pearl Harbor, thanks to sulfanilamide, no service man died from infection. Less than 4% of the compound fractures became infected, and infection did not cost any man an arm or a leg.

FIRST-AID KIT.—An adequate first-aid kit in a watertight container for a lifeboat should contain:

Adhesive tape.

Roller bandages.

Triangular bandages.

Sterile bandage compresses.

Sterile gauze squares—3" x 3".

Picric acid gauze—for burns.

Tourniquet.

Wire or thin board splints.

Scissors.

Paper cups.

Iodine—a disinfectant.

Oil of cloves—for toothache.

Aspirin—for fever.

Bismuth—for diarrhea.

Sodium bicarbonate—for burns.

5% tannic acid jelly—for burns.

Calamine lotion—for sunburn.

Mineral oil—for the eyes.

Aromatic spirits of ammonia—a stimulant.

Cascara tablets—irritant laxative; takes a minimum of water from the intestines.

ARTERIAL BLEEDING.—While someone is preparing a tourniquet, use whichever pressure point is needed to stop the bleeding. If you can prevent it, never allow bleeding to continue longer than four or five minutes.

Press your fingers on the point. Fingers may also be pressed directly on the wound, since saving a life is the primary consideration, while avoiding infection is secondary.

1. Bleeding from scalp and forehead: Press in front of the opening of the ear.
2. Bleeding from face below eyebrow: Press the side of the jaw just in front of the angle of the jawbone.
3. Bleeding from neck or throat: Put your thumb behind the neck, and the fingertips at the side of the neck beside the windpipe and press backward.
4. Bleeding from the shoulder and armpit: Press your thumb downward against the side of the neck behind the collar bone.
5. Bleeding from the arm: Press the inner side of the arm below the armpit.
6. Bleeding from the leg: Stretch the injured person out. Press the heel of your hand into the middle of the groin.

To make a tourniquet: Use a handkerchief, belt, strip of canvas, or any piece of cloth at least two inches wide. Never use a wire or a rope.

Apply the tourniquet about four inches below the armpit or groin. Take two round turns around the arm or leg and tie with a square knot. Insert a stick and twist to tighten the tourniquet. Then secure the ends of the stick.

Be sure the tourniquet is tight. You have to constrict the arteries, which are further below the surface than the veins. Loosen the tourniquet every 15 minutes by untwisting the stick. If the bleeding starts again, tighten the tourniquet.

GUNSHOT, SHRAPNEL WOUNDS.—Clean the wound— with sea water, if no other antiseptic wash is available, and you are far enough out to be certain that the water is clean. Debride the wound. That is, you must cut away all the dead and dying flesh, on which germs can feed. Your knife must be sterile—free from germs.

To sterilize the knife, either thrust the blade in the flame of a lantern or match, or dip it in the compass alcohol. The black carbon that collects on the knife from the flame will not do any harm. After sterilizing, do not touch the blade with your hands.

When you have cleaned the wound, dust it with two ounces of sulfanilamide power. To be effective, the sulfanilamide powder must be put directly onto the wound.

Place sterile gauze or layers of bandage over the wound, and bandage so that the wound will drain freely. Dressings may be sterilized by scorching. Use a heavy dressing for a chest or abdominal wound. The wound must be dressed daily.

If sulfathiazole tablets are available, they may be given by mouth to the wounded person in dosages of two 7½-grain tablets every four hours. This treatment may be continued as long as the infection shows evidence of advancing.

A mild toxic—poisonous—condition may result from the sulfathiazole treatment. This toxic condition may cause

nausea, vomiting, headache, rash, and reduced kidney function. If the toxic manifestations become pronounced, discontinue the sulfathiazole.

Due to its drying effect, suflanilamide powder checks the
healing of the wound after three or four days' treatment.
However, under lifeboat conditions, it is advisable to continue
the treatment rather than run the risk of gangrene.

FRACTURES.—Unless a simple fracture is kept immobile, it
is liable to become a compound fracture, with danger of infection which may prove fatal. Do not try to set a bone. Merely
use traction, that is, exert a slow, steady pull to straighten the
limb, turning the hand or foot to a normal position as you
pull. Then have an assistant apply splints while you maintain
traction. Except in an extreme emergency, do not move the
patient until splints are applied.

Once you have started the traction, do not release it until the
splints are in place. Thereafter, fixed traction should be used
until a doctor is reached. Fixed traction is a constant light strain
on the end of an arm or leg.

In a compound fracture put a tourniquet loosely around the
arm or leg, ready to be tightened in case of arterial bleeding.
Paint the compound fracture wound with iodine, and cover it
with a sterile dressing and bandage. If the bone is sticking out,
apply iodine to the bone as well as to the rest of the wound. No
harm is done if the protruding bone disappears when traction
is applied.

A man with a head injury should be kept lying down. The
head should be slightly raised if the face is red, but level if the
face is pale. Apply cold cloths to the head. Avoid any pressure
on the head wound. Avoid giving stimulants. Keep the person

warm. Move him only in a prone position, and avoid unnecessary handling.

SHOCK.—Shock, which may be caused by an injury, exposure, or a severe emotional disturbance, is a condition in which the fluid of the blood spreads out into the tissues. Because of this, the blood concentrates, and this concentration impedes the circulation.

The abdominal vessels dilate, thus increasing the volume of the containers of the blood. When there is more space than blood, the circulation collapses, and the victim of shock actually bleeds to death in his own circulation.

A shock victim often has a fear of impending disaster. His skin becomes clammy. He breaks out in cold perspiration, and his pulse is rapid and feeble.

In treating shock, heat applied to the abdomen or to the sides of the body is the most important. For this purpose it is advisable to purchase a chemical bag which gives off heat when water is added.

The victim should be placed on his back with his head low, so that blood will flow to the heart and brain. A teaspoonful of aromatic spirits of ammonia in half a glass of water may be given every thirty minutes. Black coffee is helpful. The patient must be kept warm and quiet.

DROWNING.—If you are swimming, never take hold of a drowning person while he is struggling. Wait until he becomes quiet. Approach him from behind. Grab his hair and pull him onto his back. Turn on your back, holding onto his hair or neck, and swim.

In the lifeboat place four oars in a row on the thwarts. Spread the life preservers on top of them, and stretch the person belly down on the preservers. You can also use the bottom of the boat by moving the bread tanks and the water breaker, but this is not advisable in a heavy sea.

Do not take time trying to get the water out of the stomach and lungs. Restore spontaneous breathing by using the simple prone-pressure method of artificial respiration. Keep it up until the person is breathing. People have regained consciousness after four hours of artificial respiration.

To restore breathing: Stretch the person, face down, full length, right arm stretched forward past the head, left arm bent. Rest the person's cheek on the bent arm.

Straddle the patient's thighs. Put your palms on each side of his back, so that pressure will work the chest like a bellows. Hold your arms straight and bear down. Squeeze all the breath out of his lungs. Hold the pressure, which should be 35 to 40 pounds and never more than 60, while you count to three. Swing back, removing the pressure completely.

The patient's lungs will expand, drawing in air. Count to three, and apply the pressure again. This action of pressure and release, pressure and release, should be repeated from 12 to 15 times a minute. Each complete movement—bearing down, then swinging back—should occupy 4 or 5 seconds.

BURNS.—Remove clothing over the burned area. If clothing sticks to the skin, cut around it, but do not attempt to remove the part that is stuck.

Apply several layers of sterile gauze soaked in a sodium bicarbonate solution, or moisten picric acid gauze and apply several layers to the burn.

Sterile gauze moistened with a 5% solution of tannic acid proves an excellent treatment. A 5% solution may be made by half-filling a sterile jar with tannic acid powder and adding fresh water after until the jar is filled.

Do not apply iodine to a burn.

A few drops of clean olive oil, mineral, or castor oil may be put into the eyes.

SUNBURN.—A lifeboat is not the place to acquire a suntan. To conserve your body's water supply, as well as to avoid sunburn, keep well covered up, especially on clear days in the tropics. Keep your clothes and hat on, and stay under the boat-cover awning as much as possible.

If you are a blond or redhead, you are far more sensitive to the sun's ultraviolet rays than if you are dark-haired. Give special consideration and protection to the heliophobe—the person who reddens and blisters, but who does not tan.

In a lifeboat your tolerance to sunshine—or the time you may safely expose yourself to the sun—is no more than 30 minutes.

The sun's reflection on the water will burn you just as severely as will the direct rays.

Even on a misty, cloudy day, it is possible to receive a painful burn.

Because of the salt on your face and body, lotions are apt to prove ineffective. If you do use a lotion, remember that many of them—and probably the one you are using—permit a 50% transmission of the sun's rays to your skin. Therefore, the lotion's value as a protective film will reach the limit of safety after one hour.

Olive oil, cocoanut oil, vinegar, carron oil—equal parts lime water and raw linseed oil—are not effective in the treatment of burns. Linseed oil and lanolin increase the possibility of infection.

Apply talcum to ease first degree burns—identified by bright redness.

For third degree burns, use tannic acid.

Pain may be eased with a 2 to 5% solution of aluminum subacetate. Apply with a compress.

SUNSTROKE.—In the doldrums, beware of sunstroke. It is caused by exposure to the sun's infrared or heat rays, with humidity and the lack of a breeze as contributing factors. Sunstroke signifies that the heat-regulating mechanism of your body has been thrown out of gear.

Your body's normal temperature is 98.6 degrees Fahrenheit. Sunstroke can run this temperature up to 113 degrees F, which is, of course, fatal.

You are not immune to sunstroke. If exposed to the sun when the air is still, African monkeys, which are used to the heat of the tropics, will soon die.

Fortunately sunstroke is almost always preceded by warnings. Headache, dizziness, spots before the eyes and swimming vision, nausea, vomiting, diarrhea, and abdominal pains indicate that you should get under cover immediately.

Loosen your clothing. Have someone fan you. Bathe your face and head. Put your wrists in sea water. Drink water in sips. Rub the skin with water to increase the circulation. Cold tea or coffee will stimulate circulation.

In case of actual sunstroke, the person should be stretched out under the awning on a bed made of the oars placed on the thwarts. Use the life preservers for cushions. Loosen the clothing. Fan him. Administer aromatic spirits of ammonia, if it is available. Have someone stand at the opposite end of the boat and dash seawater over him. Keep the patient quiet for at least forty-eight hours.

Sunstroke is dangerous. It can permanently injure the heart and brain, and it can kill.

TOOTHACHE.—If your teeth have cavities or if the nerves have given any warning of impending toothache, do not fail to take along a toothache remedy.

From the steward obtain a piece of paraffin or candle wax. Filling the cavity with paraffin will keep out salt, sugar, food, liquids, and extremes of temperature, all of which contribute to toothache.

Flooding the cavity with whiskey often will deaden the nerve, though this remedy is not always reliable.

A thick paste, consisting of zinc oxide powder mixed with a few drops of oil of cloves—both likely obtainable from the ship's medical stores—will deaden the nerve when put into the cavity.

MINOR INJURIES.—The importance of avoiding minor injuries in a lifeboat cannot be overstressed, as they will simply refuse to heal under lifeboat conditions.

Chapter 14
Morale

Do NOT UNDERVALUE morale. It is the state of mind which backs you with courage and confidence. The lack of it has proved fatal far more often than the lack of water. The lack of it has killed more seamen than bombs and torpedoes. Morale is frequently the total of little things. Do not slight the trivialities which contribute to it.

CIGARETTES.—Said Eugene Schlaflin, second engineer of the torpedoed tanker *Charles Pratt:* "Luckily we thought of cigarettes and grabbed cartons before we jumped into the boats. I think that saved some of us from going mad later."

There is magic in cigarettes. The crazed second cook who stepped over an open boat's gunwale to go "across the street to buy some pineapples" would probably be alive now if he had had cigarettes to steady him.

If you can do so without jeopardizing your safety, gather up all the cartons in the slop chest. The person in command of the boat must confiscate all cigarettes and ration them carefully. Cigarettes are most important at night to the men on watch. It is then that they supply the very essence of morale—courage and confidence.

EXTRA FOOD.—If food beyond the usual rations has been salvaged, save it for the periods of gloom. In the *Robin Moor* lifeboat, biscuit crumbs moistened with fresh water, seasoned with sea water, and mixed with canned tomatoes provided a banquet that lifted the men's spirits out of all proportion to the quality of the fare.

Boost up or reduce rations according to the prospect of reaching land. Sighting a ship is no cause for growing reckless with the food. Many vessels, fearing a submarine trap, will not stop for you.

WATER.—Though under the law water is changed periodically and the breaker is cleaned with a solution of baking soda, you may find that your supply is not as fresh as you would like it. Yet it is quite possible to make thirst-quenching in a lifeboat enjoyable.

The sparkling natural water to which you have always been accustomed has a tang due to the carbon dioxide gas it has absorbed and changed to carbonic acid. If the ship's stores yield up any bottle of charged water, bring them along. A few drops mixed with your ration of unpalatable water will restore some of its flavor.

If a man has a fever or is a diabetic, he requires more water than the others. Allow him an extra ration.

LIQUOR.—Wrote William Bligh in the log of the *Bounty's* open boat: "Being miserably wet and cold, I served to the people a teaspoonful of rum each, to enable them to bear with this distressed situation."

Liquor should be rationed out during squally weather, and to the men on watch during stormy nights.

CLOTHES.—Keep your clothes on when it rains, with dry garments under the boat cover. Even in the tropics it grows chilly during the squalls. The men on watch should have oilskins. A dead man's clothes should be distributed among the crew.

Baker, the third mate of the torpedoed *Prusa*, reported: "Any man from lifeboat #1 can tell of nights of misery beyond belief when a rain squall caught us around dark, and we huddled together all night, praying for the sun. And this was within three or four degrees of the equator."

SAILING.—Remember that the crewmen are used to a ten- or fifteen-knot ship. Unless the lifeboat is kept sailing constantly, their spirits will break. As long as the winds permit you to go in the general direction of your track, keep the boat moving.

LIGHT.—For the first couple of nights use the oil lamp. It will give the men confidence. If you have put up a rail, lash the lamp to it, securing it to prevent swinging. You can hang the lamp to the stays, providing the weather is good.

Be sure the lamp is made fast so it will not swing. A swinging lamp will have an hypnotic effect on the men looking at it. Their eyes will stray back and forth, and they will not be watching what they are doing.

NATURE.—With short rations, muscular action of the intestines is likely to be suspended. It is usually possible, therefore, with women in the boat, to take care of this need at night. The bucket is awkward; for a urinal use a small milk can.

TOOTHBRUSH.—A toothbrush not only will help you to keep your mouth from being constantly foul; but also by freshening your mouth, you will ease the sensation of thirst.

BEDDING.—Spread the life preservers on the bottom boards for those who are turning in. With two men bailing, the preservers will aid in keeping the watch below from being soaked through. Hang the preservers up daily to keep them from becoming foul.

IMPARTIALITY.—From Captain Bligh we quote a method that was time-honored even in 1789:

"I divided it (a noddy, about the size of a pigeon), with its entrails, into 18 portions, and by a well-known method of the sea, of, *who shall have this,* it was distributed, with the allowance of bread and water for dinner. . . ."

"One person turns his back on the object that it to be divided: another then points separately to the portions, at each of them asking aloud, 'Who shall have this?' to which the first answers by naming somebody. This impartial method of division gives every man an equal chance of the best share."

RECREATION.—Do not overlook books, magazines, a musical instrument. Richard Phillips, second assistant of the *Robin Moor*, took along his portable radio, and tuned in to dance music and news for the crew.

Due to the constant wetness, the deck of cards in Banigan's boat fell apart in three days. Plastic cards would have eliminated the long stretches of boredom that followed. Though more expensive, plastic cards will last longer than fifty decks of paper cards. They are not affected by salt air, water, heat, or humidity. Plastic cards are obtainable in all seaport cities.

SUICIDE.—The suicidal impulse is no stranger among open-boat crews. Yet strong clinical evidence supports the premise that seldom does a shipwrecked man, who commits suicide or has the impulse to do so, actually wish to die!

Since this is so, some understanding of the insidious trickery which the human mind can play upon its possessor may aid him to stifle the suicidal impulse.

First, the victim of hysteria. He cannot help himself. The man who suddenly starts over the side, saying, "I'm going down to the corner for a glass of beer," is suffering from hallucination, dissociation of time and place, and it is your duty to restrain him.

Our concern is with another type of suicide, the real cause of which is obscured by the apparent cause.

What of the man who goes over the side without warning, or who releases his hold on the grab line and is lost? He has sought escape, you say. He has taken a quick exit from an intolerable situation. He could not stand the rough going. Pat explanations, disproved by hundreds of case histories.

Yet the man is dead—and because of his own act. Suicide, self-destruction. True. But agreeing to that does not answer the question.

The real answer is that the man actually died because of his desire to kill an enemy. He died because of his inherent combative instinct, his inborn aggressiveness, his fighting heart!

Strange contradictions, almost unbelievable. But remember, these are facts. We are not quoting dreams.

At one time or another, every man has turned his feeling of hostility against himself. He has kicked himself, cursed himself, shaken his fist in the mirror. With our man, that *reversed hostility* has reached a fatal degree.

Unable to strike back at his foes on the U-boat, unable to revenge himself against the Japs or Nazis who blasted him from the comfort of a steamer to the hardship of an open boat, he—through a tricky mental process of which he is entirely unaware—turned his raging hatred and hostility for the foe against himself! He did not want to die. He wanted to kill!

Accept this explanation. It is backed by lifetimes of clinical research. If you become imperiled by a suicidal impulse, you can fight it down with this knowledge. It is not difficult to swing reversed hostility away from yourself. Take it out on the wind and the sea. Throw yourself into your open-boat duties. A game is a battle. If you are still bent on self-destruction, postpone the act until after a session of poker. We will wager a pretty penny that the cards will change your mind.

BURIAL AT SEA.—*Unto Almighty God we commend the soul of our brother departed, and we commit his body to the deep; in sure and certain hope of the Resurrection unto eternal* life, through our Lord Jesus Christ; at whose coming in glorious majesty to judge the world, the sea shall give up her dead; and the corruptible bodies of those who sleep in him shall be changed, and made like unto his glorious body; according to the mighty working whereby he is able to subdue all things unto himself.

Chapter 15

Water and Thirst

Your body is about 70% water. Maintaining the water balance of your body, so as to sustain life, is a far more pressing problem in an open boat than that of refueling your system.

DEPRIVATION.—If the human body is deprived of water for a few days, digestion will stop and toxic wastes will accumulate rapidly. The circulation will grow sluggish, due to the concentration of the blood, and will soon cease.

When deprived of water a person in good health will start to become delirious in about four days. Death will occur in from eight to twelve days; but at sea the shorter time is more likely.

TRUE THIRST.—The burning irritation and the sensation of dryness in the throat and mouth is Nature's signal that your body needs water.

ARTIFICIAL THIRST.—Thirst is not always due to water need. The sensation of thirst can be created by sugar and salt, and even by sweetened or salted beverages. When the water supply is scant, avoid food and drink which contain sugar or salt.

BODY HEAT.—The water in the tissues is protection against excessive body heat. When water evaporates, heat is used up. It is this process—the heat of the body being absorbed by evaporating perspiration—that keeps your body at a safe temperature.

FOOD VERSUS THIRST.—If you have no water supply, do not eat. The elimination of food wastes by the kidneys will draw water from the tissues, and will therefore reduce your survival time.

When you do eat dry food, be sure you nibble at it. The *Robin Moor* men made each biscuit last until the next ration was given out.

TEMPORARY RELIEF.—Moistening the lips and the mouth will ease the thirst sensation. Captain R.H. Cairns, master of the torpedoed British tanker *La Carrier,* allayed his thirst during the 80 hours he was in the water clinging to wreckage by chewing on the buttons from his jacket. This stimulated the flow of saliva and moistened his throat.

Chewing on a lemon rind or a piece of gum will increase the flow of saliva and give temporary relief. But this relief will not reduce your urgent need for water.

EVAPORATION.—A great amount of water is lost by the evaporation of perspiration. Keeping the body well covered, to protect the skin against the sun and wind, will lessen the body's water loss and will add to your survival time.

DOUBLE-DUTY FOODS.—In gathering your abandon-ship rations, make every possible effort to obtain double-duty foods.

Water Content of Vegetables

Sweet Potatoes, 68%

Potatoes, 77%

Kale, 86%

Onions, 87%

Beets, 87%

Carrots, 88%

Turnips, 90%

Cabbage, 92%

Spinach, 92%

Radishes, 93%

Tomatoes, 94%

Lettuce, 94%

Squash, 95%

RAIN.—*To collect rain water with the sail*: Release a stay. Bring the sail to the after part of the mast. Raise it on a slant, with men on each side. Allow the rain to clear away the salt before you begin collecting water.

After deprivation, be sure you drink in small sips. Robert Tapscott, from the torpedoed British freighter *Anglo-Saxon*, drank three canfuls of rain water after a long drought. His constricted stomach revolted and sent the water up.

BREAKERS.—If possible, double up on the breakers.

RATIONS.—Three 6-ounce cups of water a day are sufficient even in hot weather. Except for infrequent rains, each member of the crew of the *Prusa's* #1 lifeboat lived 31 days on 12 ounces of water a day.

SEA WATER.—Robert Emmett Kelly, the only survivor of a tanker torpedoed in the Caribbean, reported that his shipmates drank sea water. It made them sick and did not ease their thirst. What they did not know was that it also hastened their death.

Leslie Morgan, second cook of the torpedoed *Anglo-Saxon*, drank can after can of sea water. He went out of his mind and soon dived overboard.

Sea water has a salt content of 3½%. That is equivalent to a full teaspoon of salt in a six-ounce cup of water.

The salt content of sea water is three times greater than in human blood. Drinking sea water will exaggerate thirst, and will promote water loss through the kidneys and the intestines, thus shortening your survival time.

URINE.—Under the conditions of water deprivation, urine is too concentrated to be drunk. Its toxic waste products will add to the agony of thirst, contribute to dehydration, and lead to excessive body heat of 105 degrees and over. Drinking urine will cut down your survival time.

ALCOHOL.—Alcohol will promote water loss through the skin and kidneys. Drinking alcohol under the conditions of water deprivation is suicidal.

FATS.—A highly fat food will supply more water and cause less water loss through the kidneys than will meat or starchy foods.

When no food is consumed during water deprivation, energy must be obtained from the body's own fats and proteins. In the process of turning the body's fats and proteins into energy, water is manufactured, and this body-made water helps maintain kidney activity. Therefore, you can see that by fasting during water deprivation you will actually prolong your life.

FREEZING.—If you are in freezing weather, it is possible, provided you have a means of melting ice, to obtain water which may be safely drunk.

Put a few quarters of sea water in an air tank. The pure water will freeze first. The salt will collect in high concentration in the core of the frozen piece. Dispose of this core, which is likely to be slush ice and easy to remove, and by melting the outer portions, you will have water sufficiently free of salt to sustain life.

ICEBERGS.—When a part of a glacier reaches the sea, it breaks off and forms an iceberg. The glacial ice of a berg comes from snow, and is the source of fresh water.

FIELD ICE.—When sea water freezes, the salt is forced to the top, and during thaws and rains, this salt is washed away, leaving ice that may be melted for drinking water. To obtain fresh water at sea, last year's ice, or older, must be used.

Last year's ice
1. Rounded corners due to rains and thaws
2. Bluish in color
3. Has a glare
4. Splinters easily with knife
5. Saltiness hardly noticeable

This year's ice—Salt ice
1. Grayish in color
2. No glare
3. Tough
4. Splinters less easily
5. Salty

Chapter 16
Food and Hunger

THE POINT TO remember in selecting your extra abandon-ship rations is that your body is equipped to manufacture energy for a long time, while its water supply must be replenished frequently. If you have to choose between a food with a low calorie value but a high water content, and one that is high in energy but low in water—take the food with the water.

SURVIVAL TIME.—If you are in good health, you can live without food for as long as sixty days, though open-boat conditions probably would cut that time down to fifty days.

HUNGER.—The sensation of hunger is caused by the muscular contractions of the empty stomach. This sensation will continue throughout the period of fasting.

CALORIES.—A calorie is a unit of heat, by which the energy value of food is measured. In the doldrums your body will use up about 2000 calories a day; in rough weather, 3500 calories or more.

ENERGY VALUES.—While the water content should be your first consideration in the selection of food, it is advisable to add, if possible, some of these compact foods, which have high calorific—or energy—value. The figures given here denote calories per pound.

Jam, 1300
Condensed Milk, 1500
Cheese, 1800
Cocoa (Drink), 2100
Dried Whole Milk, 2100
Chocolate Candy, 2500
Chocolate (Drink), 2500
Milk Chocolate Candy, 2600
Cocoanut (Dried), 2600
Walnuts, 3500
Butter, 3500

WATER CONTENT.—The foods with a high water content will provide very little energy. The figures here denote calories per pound.

Onions, 90
Turnips, 100
Carrots, 200
Potatoes, 370
Canned Tomatoes, 100
Canned Carrots, 200
Canned Apricots, 470
Canned Peaches, 470
Canned Pineapple, 470

ALCOHOL.—Liquor contains considerable energy, but its function in an open boat is to sustain morale during night watches and in cold and squally weather. These figures denote calories per pint.

Gin, 1280
Whiskey, 1300
Brandy, 1350
Beer, 180

BODY FAT.—The fat in your body is stored energy. One pound of your body fat, burned up by your system, will provide 3500 calories, or sufficient energy to carry you through a day of rough weather in an open boat.

COLD WEATHER.—Sugar and fats are rapidly absorbed by the tissues, and supply a quick source of heat and energy. Foods rich in sugar and fats should be rationed during cold weather. Butter, cheese, dried milk, nuts, cocoanut, chocolate and cocoa drinks are rich in fats. Chocolate candy performs double duty, being rich in both sugar and fats.

NIGHT WATCH.—Cocoa contains a stimulant called theobromine, which resembles coffee's caffeine. On a gloomy night watch, cocoa, along with a cigarette and a ration of liquor, will prove a morale builder.

FISH SPEAR.—Should your trip be prolonged, you will often find that the water around you, particularly in the tropics, is boiling with fish.

Fishing with a hook and line is not practicable. Your hook either will be taken by a large fish, which will snap your line, or a small fish, which will be devoured before you can draw it in.

If you have a long, slender stick and a knife, you can fashion a spear which will serve you well. But do not weaken the structure of your boat by cutting away any part of it to provide your shaft.

FISH.—The flying fish which glide into your boat, and the fish you catch, may be eaten raw. But do not make Captain Bligh's mistake:

June 9, 1789
At four in the afternoon we caught a small dolphin, the first relief of the kind we obtained. I issued about two ounces to each person, including the offals, and saved the remainder for dinner the next day.

June 10, 1789
This afternoon I suffered great sickness from the oily nature of part of the stomach of the fish, which had befallen to my share at dinner.

Harold F. Dixon, the Navy filer, reported that he and his two crewmen were able to catch a small shark. They ate the shark's liver and two sardines found in its stomach, and drank the blood.

The seaweed along all the coasts supports a great population of tiny shellfish; these may be eaten.

Robert Emmett Kelly reported that one of his lifeboat mates ate a jellyfish, became deathly sick, and jumped overboard.

RAW FISH.—Bring along some bottles of lime juice. If you catch a fish, and have no means of cooking it with fire, use this Tahitian recipe. Clean the fish and cut it into small chunks. Put the chunks in a Mason jar or other glass container. Do not use tin. To one part sea water add two parts lime juice. Stir and pour over the fish, covering it entirely. Let it stand for eight hours. The citric acid will cook the fish and provide you a much-relished South Sea delicacy.

TROPICAL FISH.—Extreme care must be taken in eating fish in the tropics. In the vicinity of coral islands, for instance, nearly all the fish are at times poisonous, and the liver from one species of shark is deadly poisonous at all times.

FLYING FISH.—In areas where flying fish are plentiful, they are easily caught with a torch and a spear or a landing net. The light is thrown on the water thirty or forty feet from the boat. The fish come skipping across the water like a flat stone thrown along the surface. They will bang against the side of your boat, or fall in the water and lie blinded on the surface.

Baker, the *Prusa's* third mate, caught over 100 in one hour of fishing from a canoe near the Gilbert Islands. He used torches made of dry cocoanut leaves, and a landing net.

In a lifeboat a few may be caught by hanging a mirror, or anything that glitters, along the gunwale when the moon is bright.

DRIED FISH.—In the tropics, if water is plentiful, raw fish may be prepared by cutting them into thin slices, soaking the strips in sea water, and hanging them in the sun. This method should not be used unless water is plentiful, as the salt fish will induce thirst.

RAWHIDE.—Rawhide contains considerable food value and will not make you ill. But be sure it is rawhide. Commercially tanned leather is not to be used as food. Either boil the rawhide to a jelly-like consistency, or cut the hide into small pieces and swallow them.

PEMMICAN SOUP.—Mix your ration of pemmican with water, and heat. Then break your ration of biscuit into this soup.

DRIED SALMON.—Salmon, dried by native Alaskans, is an excellent and delicious food for Arctic weather. It is unsalted. No preservative is required except protection against the sea and rain.

SUET STEW.—Boil rice, chocolate, and chopped-up suet together in plenty of water. This was a favorite dish with the men in Stefansson's third Arctic expedition. For a day's ration: ½ lb. rice, ½ lb. suet, ¼ lb. chocolate.

To economize on fuel—bring the mixture to a boil. Then place the can on wood, a non-conductor, and wrap in a blanket. Allow the stew to cook by this fireless method for twenty minutes.

BIRDS.—The albatrosses he and his crew caught, Captain Bligh considered "not inferior in taste to fine geese." The albatross caught by the *Prusa's* crew proved to be so tough and had such a foul odor that it could not be eaten. However, the flying fish taken from its stomach were delicious.

If you have provided yourself with a slingshot, or the materials to make one, it will not take any great skill to bring down some of the birds which will fly near you.

Another method of catching birds is with a long-thonged cat-o'-nine tails.

SEAWEED.—Laver, Irish moss, and agar are used as human food; but unless you have a plentiful supply of water, you are advised against trying to obtain nourishment from seaweed. Not only are seaweeds tough and salty, but they also absorb large quantities of water, and about all you will obtain from chewing on them is an intolerable thirst.

VITAMIN DEFICIENCIES.—If your gums bleed and have a bruised appearance, you have a touch of scurvy, caused by a lack of vitamin C, which is found in fresh fruits and vegetables.

The inability to see well in a dim light indicates night blindness, the result of vitamin A deficiency. Vitamin A is found in carrots, peaches, cod liver oil, butter, eggs, milk, and beef liver.

The peeling and scaling of your skin, knee jerks and other evidences of nervousness, which may or may not be accompanied by headaches, spinal pain and melancholia, show that you are a victim of pellagra.

These symptoms are mentioned merely so you will not burden yourself with worry over the thought that you have a dangerous disease.

Scurvy, night blindness, and pellagra are the diseases of wrong diet. Soon after you reach land, proper food will cause any of these symptoms to disappear. Forget them and sail your boat.

Chapter 17

Wind and Rain

THE INFORMATION IN this chapter is chiefly to help guide you if the Pilot Chart has been lost from your lifeboat. It will give you some knowledge of what winds you may expect in your latitude, so that you will not be misled by a short variation from the prevailing wind.

The rainy seasons are given to guide you in the rationing of water.

If the prevailing wind is blowing in the direction of enemy territory, the section on the rigging and use of a spritsail is of vital importance to you.

PILOT CHART.—For the price, you cannot obtain more information regarding winds than from a U.S. Hydrographic Office Pilot Chart. Again you are urged to provide yourself with Pilot Charts—at 10¢ a sheet—as insurance against the possibility of the chart in your lifeboat being lost.

To understand the information on the Pilot Chart, no knowledge of meteorology is needed. Knowing your approximate position, you will be able to find out the average velocities of winds in your vicinity, and their directions. The trade wind boundaries are distinctly marked.

BEAUFORT SCALE.—You will need this scale in reading the wind roses on the Pilot Charts. The number of feathers on a wind-rose arrow shows the average force of the wind on the Beaufort scale.

Force	Wind	Velocity, miles per hour
0	Calm	Less than 1
1	Light Air	1–3
2	Light Breeze	4–7
3	Gentle Breeze	8–12
4	Moderate Breeze	13–18
5	Fresh Breeze	19–24
6	Strong Wind	25–31
7	High Wind (mod. gale)	32–38
8	Gale	39–46
9	Strong Gale	47–54
10	Whole Gale	55–63
11	Storm	64–75
12	Hurricane	Over 75

TRADE WINDS.—The trade winds are steady winds which blow constantly in the same direction. They are caused by differences in temperature between the polar and equatorial regions.

The trade winds blow from subtropical belts of high pressure toward equatorial belts of low pressure. These belts encircle the earth, and range from 3 degrees N to 35 degrees N, and from the Equator to 28 degrees S. They make seasonal shifts north and south.

The heat of the equatorial region causes the air to rise. Surface currents from cool north and south latitudes flow into the equatorial region, replacing the ascending warm air.

In the North Atlantic, from 20 degrees N to 30 degrees N, south of the Azores and west of Madeira, the NE trade winds blow strongly in summer. These NE trades are especially strong near the Canaries and the Antilles, and can be felt as far north as Gibraltar.

The SE trades blow weakly in the summer months. They are strong during winter, especially along the North Brazilian Coast.

MEAN LIMITS.—The limits of the trade winds vary each quarter—every three months.

For instance, the mean—or average—of the southern limit of the NE trades is 2 degrees N during the first three months of the year, 4 degrees N the second quarter, 10 degrees N the third quarter, and 6 degrees N during the last quarter.

The northern mean limit ranges from 25 degrees N to 30 degrees N, and decreases for the last half of the year.

If you lack a Pilot Chart, you can apply the above variations to the following mean limits to determine approximately how far the trade winds in your area, and in whatever season you are sailing, will take you.

North Atlantic
  Southern Belt 2° N–10° N
  Northern Belt 25° N–30° N
South Atlantic
  Southern Belt 30° S–25° S
  Northern Belt 0°–5° N
North Pacific
  Southern Belt 8° N–12° N
  Northern Belt 25° N–30° N
South Pacific
  Southern Belt 30° S–25° S
  Northern Belt 4° N–8° N
South Indian
  Southern Belt 30° S–25° S
  Northern Belt 15° S–0°

MONSOONS.—The monsoons are winds which blow over the Arabian Sea, Bay of Bengal, China Sea, and along the coasts of Asia. The NE or dry monsoon blows in winter; the SW or wet monsoon blows in summer.

DOLDRUMS.—The doldrums in equatorial belts are areas where light airs, calms, clouds, and rain prevail.

HORSE LATITUDES.—When the heated, rising currents of air of the equatorial region reach an altitude above that of the polar atmosphere, these currents form a horizontal current which flows toward the poles, just as water flows downhill.

In the temperate latitudes this current of air cools; in the horse latitudes are some descending air currents, fine weather, light and variable winds. The equalizing of atmospheric pressure in these regions results in a calm.

That is why, in the Tropics of Cancer and Capricorn, you may come upon large ocean areas where there is no wind for days.

WESTERLIES.—Westerlies are the prevailing winds you will encounter in the high latitudes. However, you may at times encounter winds blowing north and south; but the general average in high latitudes will be Westerlies.

The high pressure belt in the south contributes strong NW to W winds over an area from 35 degrees S to 65 degrees S. These Westerlies are encountered around the Horn and the Cape of Good Hope. This area, in which storms are frequent, has been dubbed the "Roaring Forties."

In the corresponding latitudes of the North Atlantic and North Pacific, Westerlies also prevail.

SPRITSAIL.—If you are near enemy territory and find that the wind is carrying you in that direction, it is advised that you change your lug sail into a spritsail.

A sprit will allow you to point a little higher to the wind, which will enable you to tack to better advantage than is possible with a lug. However, with a sprit you will not make much speed. For a long distance use a lug sail.

To change the lug sail to a sprit: Remove the yard. Sew a piece of canvas across the peak—the after top corner of the sail—so as to form a pocket. Bend the halyard onto the nock—the forward top corner of the sail.

Bend two or three lengths of marlin or grommets to the luff of the sail, and fit them around the mast.

With 9 or 12 thread make a snotter—a short line with an eye splice on each end.

Make two round turns or a clove hitch around the mast with the snotter—so that the eyes come together.

Fit the blade of your steering oar into the pocket. Put the handle of the oar through the eyes of the snotter.

Bend the tack—the lower forward corner of the sail—to the mast and secure.

Haul in the slack of the sheet.

Now you have afore-and-aft sail which will allow you to tack with much more efficiency than with a lug.

RAINFALL.—In rationing your water, it is well to remember that you may have squalls all around you, without a bit of rain coming your way.

RAINY SEASONS.—The following list is given to help you in the rationing of water on a long open-boat trip. You may find yourself short of water in one of these areas, and with no sign of water in the sky, even though the rainy season may be about to start.

Caribbean Sea, June
Brazil, northern, January to April
Brazil, May to September
West Indies, July to October
Africa, west coast, S of equator, November to April

Africa, west coast, N of equator, May to October
Hawaiian Islands, December to April
Ecuadorean coast, December to April
South Pacific Islands, November to April
Mexico, Central America, June to October
Arabian Sea, May to September
Bay of Bengal, May to September
China Sea, May to September

Chapter 18

Freezing Weather

YOUR BEST INSURANCE against exposure and frostbite is a life suit. If you are wearing heavy underclothing, a life suit will keep you warm in the coldest weather. Ten persons died from exposure in a *City of New York* lifeboat. Life suits undoubtedly would have saved several of them, and perhaps the entire ten.

The seamen from the torpedoed Norwegian motor tanker *Alexandra Hoegh* were rescued after 38 hours in open boats during midwinter in the North Atlantic. They reached shore well and healthy. All of them would have been frostbitten, and some of them would have died—if they had not worn life suits.

FROSTBITE.—Frostbite is a mild term for a very serious and painful affliction. Robert N. Peck, who survived the *City of New York* torpedoing, suffered second degree frostbite, characterized by blisters and a deeply reddened skin. For weeks he was unable to get a night's sleep, and he was incapacitated for three months.

Frostbite is caused by the action of cold on the body tissues. This action blocks the circulation and deprives the affected area of its blood supply.

DEGREES OF FROSTBITE.—1st: skin dark-red; affected area painful. 2nd: skin bright red or livid blue; blisters. 3rd: affected area white, stiff, brittle; danger of gangrene.

CONTRIBUTING CAUSES.—Fatigue is foremost among the contributing causes to frostbite, due to the vitality being lowered and the circulation slowed. Hunger, malnutrition, and vitamin deficiency increase one's susceptibility to frostbite.

WIND.—Wind increases the danger of frostbite. In a lifeboat a windbreak should be rigged, and everyone should be kept under the boat cover as much as possible.

MOISTURE.—Chilling through wet clothing will cause frostbite more quickly than if the cold reaches the body through dry garments.

PERSPIRATION.—Though waterproof shoes should be worn, they retain the perspiration, which will hasten frostbite.

GREASE.—Grease spread over the body will not protect you from the cold. Grease will make your clothes less protective by filling the air pockets, which are the real sources of warmth. In a high wind, grease on the face will prove helpful, but it is useless in still cold. A small amount of oil may be applied to the feet, and rubbed in until the surface is dry. A large quantity will prove harmful.

CLOTHING.—Warmth from your clothing is supplied by the air pockets between the fibers and the air layers between the layers of clothing. These air layers prevent too much heat from getting out and too much cold from getting in. Clothing should not constrict. Avoid tight garters and tight shoes. Loosen the shoe strings. Wear two or more pairs of socks—woolen over cotton.

WOOL AND FUR.—Woolens and furs offer excellent protection against the cold because non-conducting air pockets are formed in the meshes, and these air pockets provide insulation between the skin and the outer temperature.

HAIR.—Excellent protection against cold is provided by the hair on your head.

BEARD.—Moisture from the breath will congeal on the beard, forming a face mask separated from the skin by one-eighth of an inch of air space. If your face begins to freeze, you may not know it. The ice mask will make it difficult to get to the cheek to warm it with your hand. Keep clean-shaven.

TOBACCO.—Tobacco tightens the blood vessels and increases the susceptibility to frostbite by decreasing the circulation.

COFFEE.—Coffee also tightens the blood vessels, and will further reduce the lowered temperature of the affected part.

SYMPTOMS.—By making grimaces, you can detect any stiff spot on your face. Those in a lifeboat should watch one another for signs of frostbite. Be on the alert for these signs:

1. Drop in circulation. If the skin does not whiten when you press it with your finger, the blood supply is below normal.
2. Loss of heat. Determine this by touching an exposed part and a protected area. If the affected part feels colder, frostbite has set in.
3. Numbness. The loss of sensation is extremely dangerous, because the frostbite may eat into the flesh to the bone without you knowing it.
4. Lessened function of the part, or the inability to use them.
5. Color changes. A red and purple mottled appearance is evidence of frostbite. In an advanced stage, the part becomes gray-white.

TREATMENT.—Restoring circulation to injured tissues should be done in gradual stages. Warm the frostbitten area against a part of your own body.

Face: Warm with your hand.

Wrist: Grasp wrist with the other hand.

Hand: Place on naked chest or under the armpit.

Foot: Place against naked part of a companion's body.

In first degree frostbite, the part may be rubbed gently. There must be no rubbing in more severe frostbite. If possible, apply cold cloths, raising the temperature a degree or two every few minutes.

After circulation has been restored, apply boracic acid ointment, or an ointment composed of Vaseline one ounce, camphor
six grains. The blisters should be pricked with a needle, but do
not remove the skin. Cover with cotton or flannel cloths.

If gangrene has set in, wet cloths with alcohol and place
over the affected part to prevent infection.

BOAT COVER.—In freezing weather the cover must not be
taken off the boat. Rain or snow freezing in the bottom of the
boat will make it difficult or impossible to put in the plug, and
will freeze fast other gear so as to hinder you.

WATER BREAKER.—To keep the water in the breaker from
freezing, remove the plug. Insert a stick in the breaker. The
lower end of the stick should be weighted, and the upper end
should protrude a foot or more. The movement of the ship will
keep the stick in motion so that ice will not be able to form.
In port, put the breakers in the fidley to keep the water from
freezing.

FROZEN FOOD.—If you are in freezing weather, it is advisable to have certain foods prepared and stored in the reefer,
ready to be transferred to the lifeboat.

Potatoes, eggs, and apples may be kept frozen, but they must
be used as soon as they are thawed.

Milk is convenient to handle if frozen in bricks or cubes.

Cut meat into steaks or small roasts before freezing.
Frozen meat may be cut with an ax or a saw. Save the meat
splinters and sawdust.

Bacon fat is delicious, and in extreme cold it will freeze clean
so that your mittens will be no more than slightly stained in

handling it. At zero butter is clean to handle, while at 30 below lard may be handled in chunks.

Baked beans may be frozen in bricks, but beans will be easier to heat if you bake them dry and freeze them in separate kernels. Put a little water or grease in your can, pot, or cup, and warm them over a canned heat fire. Beans baked with pork will keep for several months, though the pork may have a slightly rancid taste.

MEAT.—For one year Stefansson lived entirely on meat and water. He found that 1⅓ lbs. of lean and ½ lb. of fat daily were sufficient.

FAT.—Fat is the top heat-producer because it is quickly absorbed into the tissues, and has more calories per unit of weight than any other food. If you are deprived of sugar and starch, you will soon develop a taste for fat, unless you are the one person in a hundred who cannot eat it. You can die from continued overeating of lean, but your digestive system will prevent you from overeating fat.

PROTEIN POISONING.—Many men in the Arctic have died of starvation, despite a plentiful supply of meat. A diet of rabbit alone, for instance, will leave you hungry no matter how much you eat. In a few weeks a person trying to subsist on such a diet will die of protein poisoning.

You cannot live on lean meat alone. You must have fat. Cranes, owls, ravens, and ptarmigan have insufficient fat.

POLAR BEAR.—If you are in the Arctic regions armed with a high-powered gun, you may find it possible to shoot a polar bear. The bear will not be able to see you at a distance greater than 300 yards. You should use soft-nosed bullets, and your aim should be for a place just behind the shoulder, so that the bullet will pierce the heart. Do not shoot a polar bear while it is in the water. You will not be able to haul it out.

It is advisable to eat bear meat raw and frozen, or half frozen. Bear meat becomes stringy when it is cooked. It will get between the teeth and make the gums sore. Avoid polar bear liver. Sometimes it is slightly poisonous, and will cause vomiting and give you a bad headache.

CARIBOU.—The choice part of a caribou is the head. The ribs, neck, shoulders, heart and kidneys are eaten. The natives feed the liver and sweetbreads to the dogs. The fats may be dried, and the marrow is eaten raw.

SEAL.—Seals are to be found under sea ice, on top of it, and in open water between floes. Most seals shot in the head will float. With body wounds, three out of ten will be lost.

All parts of the seal, except the entrails, may be eaten. The heart and kidneys are choice. The liver may be boiled or eaten raw.

Appendix

Abstract of Banigan's Voyage in a *Robin Moor* Lifeboat

MAY 21—NO attempt to sail. Put out sea anchors, drifted, rested, kept clear of wreckage. Night, boats secured by painters. Mast stepped. Lantern set up. Men in #4, on tail end, rowed to keep other boats apart.

May 22—Old Man's orders to sail for St. Paul Rocks, light, unwatched. Sailed 0815 GMT. 14 mi. to noon. Mod. NE wind, sea and swell. Set watches, 3 on a watch. Instructed men how to steer. Lengthened stays with lifeline. Added canvas to get more sail area. Rations 3 times day: 1 biscuit, 1 cup water, ½ small onion. Night, signaled to Old Man with flares.

May 23—71 mi. to noon. Rain squalls. Overcast. Knocked out end of air tank to catch rain water. Made tiller out of spreaders. Yoke with lanyards inefficient.

May 24—43 mi. to noon. Made new sea anchor. Night, permission from Old Man to go off alone. Taylor rowed off with his boat and disappeared over horizon. NE wind. Mod. NE sea and swell. Near southernmost limit NE trades. Realize cannot make St. Paul Rocks.

May 25—41 mi. to noon. Overcast, heavy rain squalls. Rough SE sea and mod. swell. Mod. SE wind.

May 26—67 mi. to noon. Overcast, heavy rain squalls. Mod. SE wind. Rough sea and heavy swell. Current setting to northwestward. Wind abeam. Afternoon, Hugh Murphy, messboy, at tiller, almost ran aboard two whales. Night, heavy squalls. Blowing. All but three men on weather side. Last attempt to make south latitude. Flares seen from the other boats. Answered. Taylor's boat reappeared. Shipping water, bailing constantly. Cold. Rationed liquor.

May 27—64 mi. to noon. Rough and heavy sea. Almost got swamped. Told men could not make Rock. Current, wind, sea setting us off. Decided to run before it. Faces fell. Night, following sea. A.B.'s steering.

May 28—101 mi. to noon. Rough sea, heavy swell. Partly cloudy. Too far northward, tried to make something. Men well, but wet, chilled.

May 29—67 mi. to noon. Rain squalls. Mod. SE wind. Heavy sea and swell.

May 30—30 mi. to noon. Overcast. Light var. airs. When sun came out, burned through clothes. Feet and legs swelled. Night, boat pounded.

May 31—No sight. Drifted. Overcast. Terrific burns. Water boiling with fish. Men restless.

June 1—36 mi. to noon. Overcast, rain squalls. Mod. SE swell. Light airs. Night, NW winds, died out in morning.

June 2—69 mi. to noon. Morning, smoke spotted. Saw ship for 5 hrs. About 7 mi. off, changing course. Rags burned, kerosene smudge, but smoke blended with clouds. Cook crying, panicking others. Men rowed. Let them row one hour. Night, no wind. Pounded.

June 3—No observation. Water alive with fish. Drifted. Heavy SE sea and swell. Heavy rain squalls.

Light var. airs. Terrific pounding. Shivered all day and night. Lack of cigarettes felt.

June 4—79 mi. from noon of 2nd. Light var. winds to light airs. Overcast. Mod. swell. Heavy rain squalls.

June 5—17 mi. to noon. Overcast, cloudy. Heavy rain. Lt. airs, mod. SE swell. Night, crew getting leery.

June 6—27 mi. to noon. Cloudy, clear. Gentle to mod. SE wind. Mod. rough sea and swell.

June 7—52 mi. to noon. Gentle to mod. SE wind and mod. rough sea. Cloudy and clear.

June 8—73 mi. to noon. Mod. E'ly winds. Partly cloudy and clear. Rough sea and swell. 35 mi. from Great Circle track. Men excited. Watched steering. Sharp lookout. Night, moonlight. Seas became very rough. Decided to get nap and then stay up rest of night. 9:45, Peter Buss, A.B., reported light. Sent up flare. Got men on oil lamp. Men jumped on thwarts. Lifted center of gravity, almost capsized. Light over side of ship. Hove to. Came about, got alongside. Brazilian ship, *Osorio*. Got men aboard. Holes cut in tanks and bottom of lifeboat to sink it. Dist. 898 mi. Total time—18 days, 16 hrs., 49 mins.